Rue Marcadet, Paris, *18th arrondissement*

JILL O'CONNOR    *Photographs by Richard Eskite* >>

# Simple French Desserts

CHRONICLE BOOKS

SAN FRANCISCO

Library of Congress Cataloging-in-Publication
Data:

O'Connor, Jill.
    Simple French Desserts / by Jill O'Connor:
    photographs by Richard Eskite.
    p. cm.
    ISBN 0-8118-1903-5 (pb.)
    1. Desserts—France.
    2. Cookery, French.  I. Title
    TX773.O318        2000
    641.8'6'0944—dc21
    99-31921          CIP

Printed in Hong Kong.

Prop styling by Sara Slavin
Food styling by Sandra Cook
Designed by Jeremy Stout
Illustrations by Get It Design
The photographer wishes to thank:
    Kevin Hossler, Juliann Harvey,
    Vicki Roberts-Russell, Emily Dolan,
    and Sarah Dawson.

Distributed in Canada by Raincoast Books
8680 Cambie Street
Vancouver, British Columbia V6P 6M9

10 9 8 7 6 5 4 3 2 1

Chronicle Books
85 Second Street
San Francisco, California 94105

www.chroniclebooks.com

**DEDICATION**

To Jim, for all your great advice, love, and support. Thank you for always listening, and for never, ever saying "I told you so."

**ACKNOWLEDGMENTS**

Many thanks to my editor, Bill LeBlond, for his patience and understanding as I worked my way through this manuscript. I would also like to thank Leslie Jonath, whose advice is always appreciated. Hugs and kisses to my husband, Jim, and daughter, Olivia, who at the height of my recipe testing, remained enthusiastic and never complained if they were served crème caramel for breakfast, or macaroni and cheese and four different kinds of chocolate mousse for dinner.

Denise Kuhn and Anna Jacobsen, my taste-testers *extraordinaire*, provided me with great advice and comments as they threw caution, and all thoughts of their waistlines, to the wind and fearlessly ate every tart, custard, and cookie I set before them.

Most of all, I want to thank my great friend and traveling companion, Mary Ann Kelly, who trudged through the streets of Paris with me, wandering in and out of countless pâtisseries and bistros, in search of the creamiest crème caramel, the best macaroons, and the finest financiers and madeleines. Thanks for your terrific sense of humor and your peerless sense of direction!

# CONTENTS

# $\mathscr{I}$NTRODUCTION

**I LOVE FOOD AND I LOVE TO COOK,** but I especially love to read about food, since it involves two of my favorite things: books and lolling on my couch. I love to read about people who grow twenty-seven varieties of heirloom tomatoes and all their own herbs; who summer in Italy, drinking cool glasses of *prosecco* under a hot Tuscan sun. Curled up on my own couch, I can shop vicariously with the author, meandering through a Provençal market perfumed with the heady aroma of nearby lavender fields, filling my string bag with fresh figs and local honey, then carrying my goodies home to a kitchen whose long counters are lined with antique *confit* pots and pitchers holding a tangle of whisks and wooden spoons.

Unfortunately, I don't have a villa in Tuscany, nor have I fulfilled my fantasy of owning a farmhouse in Provence where I can retire to raise goats and thump Charentais melons into the twilight of my years. In fact, I really have no idea what kind of kitchen is in my near future. In the past twelve years, I have moved nine times, with another move looming as I write this introduction. My husband is a commander in the Navy, and we have lived in places as diverse and exciting as London, Japan, Hawaii, and my native California. Resettling in all these different places has been in turns exciting, thrilling, frustrating, and lonely, but never dull, and always a culinary adventure. Over the years, I've cooked in many strange and daunting kitchens; I've tamed an electric stove that seemed to have only two temperatures—off and scalding Hell-fire hot—

balanced food in a refrigerator with an interior narrow enough to challenge Houdini, and baked dozens of Christmas cookies six at a time in a toaster oven. In Japan we had a very tiny kitchen; working in it always felt like a surreal cross between camping and cooking in Barbie's dream kitchen. In this pint-sized kitchen we had two gas burners to cook on with a miniature fish broiler (de rigueur in most Japanese kitchens) beneath the burners. A skeptic, I never prepared anything more complicated than toast in the fish broiler. Beneath the fish broiler was a miniature combination convection-microwave oven. Since the directions were all in kanji, the only time I could tell whether I had started the convection oven instead of the microwave was when I melted the plastic wrap covering the food I was trying to reheat. Through lots of trial and error—and melted plastic—I finally mastered operating it. On Christmas day, I even managed to cook a crown roast of pork in the tiny oven. I had to roast it upside down, and it completely filled the oven, but it worked!

Like many people, I've had to cook in kitchens that would never be featured in *House Beautiful* or grace the pages of any cooking magazine. Although I've lusted after gleaming six-burner, dual-heat Viking ranges, dreamed of countertops lined with South American granite, and an endless butcher-block island sporting a pastry center lined with marble perfect enough to make Michelangelo weep (all of it lit, of course, in the flawless glow of discreetly recessed pure white halogen lights), I've never let the absence of this culinary Xanadu stop me or slow me down, and neither should you. I know it is possible to create beautiful, satisfying food in even the most challenging circumstances, with the most fundamental equipment and with ingredients available to the most basic cook.

After all my travels, I am still besotted with French food, especially the desserts and pastries. Wandering into one of the many pâtisseries that dot the streets and boulevards of Paris will enchant anyone with a sweet tooth. Entering a French pâtisserie is like walking into a jewel box, where the *charlottes aux fruits rouges* glisten like rubies next to sleek lemon tarts, stately saverins, and ornate gâteaux, romantically christened with names like *magie noire, marjolaine,* or *jour et nuit.* Colorful macaroons in pastel shades of pistachio green, raspberry pink, and mocha line up next to rich almond financiers, named for the gold bricks they resemble. Elegant chocolate-glazed éclairs, cream puffs, and cloudlike meringues sandwiched with cream sing their irresistible siren song to hungry shoppers from behind clear glass windows. Buttery sablés and lemony

madeleines round out an overwhelmingly luxurious and glittering array of sumptuous treats. The masterpieces highlighted in the pâtisserie's shop windows feature the fruits of the French pastry chef's formidable art.

Which leads us to the title of this book, *Simple French Desserts.* Preparing desserts, especially desserts culled from the rich and complex world of the French pâtisserie, strikes fear in the hearts of many cooks, especially inexperienced or busy ones. *Simple French Desserts* will change all that. Although the rich variety of desserts available in the French pastry shop may seem daunting to re-create, many of them are fairly simple to make at home. Desserts available in busy bistros and brasseries include classic, simple but satisfying custards, tarts, puddings and ice creams that any busy cook can create at home. There is a term in French, *à la ménagère,* or "housewife style," that refers to simple, everyday dishes prepared with common ingredients accessible to any good housewife. *À la ménagère* definitely describes most of the recipes in *Simple French Desserts.* If you can pick up a whisk, plug in a mixer, separate an egg, or roll out a pie crust, there are simple, yet elegant French desserts within your grasp.

The recipes in this book are classics. Common, but often unexplained, cooking techniques are highlighted throughout the book in colorful sidebars. Everything from melting chocolate and making caramel to beating egg whites and poaching fruit is explained in a clear, uncomplicated way.

Many elaborate-looking French desserts are as simple to create as all-American brownies or butterscotch pudding, while delivering flavors that are subtle and sophisticated. *Simple French Desserts* is for the home baker who has more desire than time, and more determination than training. The busy mother who wants to prepare a simple French dessert during those precious few hours called "naptime" will find the answer in the pages of this book. Desserts like crisp, airy meringues, or a rustic Basque cake hiding a sour cherry filling, can be prepared in just a few minutes with ingredients found in most American pantries and refrigerators.

*Simple French Desserts* holds the answers for the first-time host who wants to treat his or her guests to an elegant, homemade dessert when the only equipment in the kitchen is the oven, a few stainless steel mixing bowls, and a whisk bought at the grocery store. Coeur à la crème or luscious pots de crème can be prepared without any fancy equipment and with a minimum of fuss. Many recipes can be prepared at least one day in advance, giving a nervous host one less thing to worry about.

This book is for people who want to simplify their cooking without simplifying their menu. You can create a great dessert within the rich tradition of French cooking without going to cooking school to do it. *Simple French Desserts* will demystify even seemingly complex French desserts by explaining the techniques required to execute them successfully. I hope this volume of recipes will inspire you to expand your culinary horizons. Cooking is a creative skill that I believe is important to demonstrate and pass on to our children. The simple pleasures of the kitchen are a vital part of life, and good food brings a sense of respite, community, and continuity into the busiest of lives. Learning to cook is an adventure, and mastering the skills, simple techniques, and recipes outlined in this book will increase your confidence and your enjoyment of this very practical art.

## How to Use This Book

Baking is as much a science as an art, so organization is a key to success. Assemble all the equipment and ingredients necessary for the recipe before you begin. Make sure the oven is preheated, if necessary, and that you have cleared room in your freezer or refrigerator to chill or store your finished dessert. If you read a recipe that requires a piece of equipment you don't have, you can often substitute something else. You can substitute mini-muffin tins for madeleine or financier pans, or use oven-safe coffee cups instead of custard cups or ramekins. If you try a recipe and like it, consider investing in the proper piece of equipment. Using the right equipment for the job will increase your enjoyment and success, and the equipment specified in this volume is neither expensive nor difficult to find.

# Equipment

You don't need a huge variety of equipment to prepare most of the recipes in this book. The following list of equipment includes absolute necessities plus the pieces that make baking easier and so much more enjoyable, should you choose to invest in them. Starting with the most basic tools and working up to the larger, more expensive, or less versatile items, this "wish list" is good to have when building a proper *batterie de cuisine*.

**Measuring cups:** Use individual metal cups in 1-cup, 1/2-cup, 1/3-cup, and 1/4-cup sizes. They are more accurate for measuring dry ingredients than 8-ounce or 16-ounce glass measuring cups, preferred for liquids.

**Oven thermometer:** A crucial bit of equipment, as oven temperatures can be wildly off. An oven thermometer ensures that you are baking at the proper temperature.

**Stainless steel mixing bowls:** These come in a wide variety of sizes and are inexpensive, durable, lightweight, heat resistant, and versatile. They can be heated, chilled, and frozen with absolutely no problems; they won't break or chip like ceramic bowls or melt in the dishwasher like plastic bowls. Available everywhere, from exclusive kitchenware stores to restaurant supply stores, discount stores like Wal-Mart and K-Mart, and even some grocery stores, these bowls will become the workhorses of your kitchen.

**Knives:** A good-quality paring knife and an 8-inch or 10-inch chef's knife will take you anywhere in the culinary world you want to go.

**Wooden spoons:** Inexpensive and versatile, wooden spoons feel good in your hand and have just the right heft and shape for stirring ingredients together. Purchase one or two and use them instead of plastic spoons (they won't melt) or metal spoons (they won't scrape or damage your pots and pans).

**Rubber or heatproof silicone spatula:** Heatproof silicone is a recent improvement over the old-fashioned rubber spatula. It won't stain or absorb flavors and can withstand higher temperatures than rubber can without melting. Spatulas made from either material are priceless for folding ingredients together and scraping batters from bowls. Invest in at least one large flat spatula and one of the newer spoon-shaped varieties for versatility.

**Parchment paper/Silpat sheets:** Crucial for keeping cookies from sticking and for lining cake pans. Using parchment paper relieves so much stress in the kitchen, it is worth seeking out and having on hand as you would foil or plastic wrap. Silpat, a new nonstick, washable, and reusable material from France, is used to make baking sheet liners, and for financier and madeleine molds.

**Wire whisks:** Available in a wide variety of sizes. You should have at least one large, round balloon whisk for whipping air into foods including egg whites, sauces, and cream. A longer, narrower whisk with stiffer wires, sometimes called a "piano whisk," is useful for beating heavier ingredients together and preventing lumps from forming when preparing a custard or sauce.

**Box grater:** The smallest holes on this type of grater are used to grate citrus zest.

**Zester:** A tool for creating long, delicate ribbons of orange, lemon, and lime zest–fast.

**Melon baller:** Use for coring pears and apples and, of course, for making melon balls.

**Fruit and vegetable peeler:** A swivel peeler with a rubber handle is best for removing peels from apples and pears and for cutting large strips of citrus zest.

**Electric hand mixer:** This inexpensive kitchen basic is a must if you want to easily prepare a cake batter, or whip cream or egg whites. Even if you have one of the larger, free-standing mixers, a smaller hand mixer is often more convenient for mixing or beating together smaller quantities of ingredients.

**Saucepans:** It is worth investing in a small set of heavy, stainless steel–lined pans in these sizes and shapes: a 1-quart, 2-quart, and 3-quart saucepan; a deep 12-inch skillet or wok for deep-frying; and an 8-inch nonstick skillet or French crêpe pan for preparing crêpes.

**Rolling pin:** Either a spinning one with handles, or one of the large "French" pins without handles (they resemble large dowels). Both work well, so it just depends on what you feel more comfortable using.

**Baking sheets:** You should have at least two heavy professional aluminum baking sheets, called "half sheets," available in restaurant supply stores and kitchenware shops. They are versatile and inexpensive. Invest in at least one insulated baking sheet. These baking sheets diffuse the heat of the oven and protect the bottom of the cookie or pastry you are baking from browning excessively (Cushionaire is a popular brand). They are perfect for delicate sablé cookies, but are less successful with pâte à choux pastries and macaroons, which need more direct exposure to oven heat to rise properly. If you don't want to invest in an insulated baking sheet, or your baking sheets are not very heavy, try "double-panning": Simply place a second baking sheet of the same size under the first and bake as directed.

**Piping bags:** The most durable are made from plastic-coated cloth. One 16-inch and one 18-inch bag are good sizes to start with.

**Icing spatulas and an offset spatula:** Thin, flexible metal spatulas with a rounded tip come in various lengths—6 inches, 8 inches, and 12 inches—to use for icing cakes, spreading fillings, and so on. Offset spatulas have an angled blade, making them perfect for removing small and delicate items from baking sheets and angling into tight spots.

**Sieve:** For straining custards, sifting flour, cocoa, and confectioners' sugar. Metal sieves are the most useful for quickly sifting dry ingredients. Fine-meshed and plastic-meshed sieves are good for straining custards; they won't cause the custard to discolor or give it a metallic aftertaste.

**Pastry Brush:** A natural boar-bristle brush with a wooden handle is best for brushing glazes on tarts and cookies and pastry dough. Buy two: one for using with melted butter, and one for egg washes and fruit glazes.

**Fluted quiche or tart pans with removable bottoms:** You should have at least one 9$\frac{1}{2}$-inch tart pan and four 4$\frac{3}{4}$-inch tartlet pans.

**White porcelain custard cups and ramekins:** Heavy, heat-resistant, white "bistroware" custard cups and ramekins for a wide variety of custards and puddings. Start with at least six 6-ounce custard cups or ramekins and work up to a collection of eight of each.

**Straight-sided cake pans:** Inexpensive, heavy-duty aluminum pans 2 or 3 inches deep are available in restaurant supply stores, kitchenware stores, or anywhere cake-decorating supplies are sold. Great for cakes (of course), but also for bread puddings and cheesecakes. You can even line them with plastic wrap and use them as a mold for chocolate mousse. Purchase two each in 8-inch, 9-inch, and 10-inch sizes.

**Spring-form pan:** A straight-sided cake pan with removable sides. Necessary for soft or delicate cakes like cheesecakes and the chocolate soufflé cake in this book.

**Double boiler:** Handy for melting chocolate and cooking the orange and lemon cream in this book.

**Roasting pan or 9-by-13-inch baking pan:** For use as a water bath for desserts as well as for roasting.

**Loaf pan:** An 8½-by-4½-inch loaf pan for tea cakes and pound cakes.

**Financier molds:** A pan with 2-by-4-inch molds. The romance of baking little French cakes in the proper pan can't be beat. If you develop a love for easy-to-bake financiers, it's worth searching for a financier mold.

**Madeleine pan:** A metal pan with twelve shell-shaped molds.

**Coeur à la crème mold:** A white porcelain heart-shaped mold with holes in the bottom for draining whey from this classic French fresh-cheese dessert. Not necessary, but it does give a pleasing and classic shape to this traditional dessert.

**Mini propane or butane blowtorch:** To caramelize crèmes brûlées, fruit tarts, or soft meringue.

## "Big Ticket" Equipment

**Free-standing mixer:** I could write an ode to my KitchenAid mixer. If stranded on a desert island, I'd want it with me. It makes life so much easier and I think it is the single most important piece of equipment a baker can own; it tirelessly mixes doughs, beats egg whites, buttercreams, and cake batters, freeing your hands to finish other tasks and preventing your arms from aching. With a paddle attachment for cookie and pastry doughs, a whisk attachment to beat egg whites and cream, and more, a free-standing mixer pays for itself a hundred times over. Depending on the size you choose and where you purchase your mixer, they can range in price from $200 to $400. Definitely an investment, but if you plan on doing much baking, you'll never be sorry.

**Food processor:** Perfect for chopping nuts and creating "nut flours," pureeing fruit, and preparing various cookie and pastry doughs, the food processor has become a staple of the kitchen. Inexpensive mini processors are also available and can do most of the chores accomplished by the larger, more expensive models. They are easier to store and just as versatile for small amounts of ingredients.

**Blender:** A blender can do many of the tasks of a food processor. Not only does the blender make the best margaritas and milkshakes, it is the perfect tool for pureeing fruit, blending sauces, and preparing crêpe batter.

**Ice cream maker:** If you have a yen for homemade ice cream, there are a variety of models available, from the old-fashioned hand-cranked version, to an electric version that uses ice and rock salt. My favorite models, and the easiest to use, are small, electric sealed-coolant versions. The container is frozen overnight, which eliminates the need for ice and salt. They are reasonably priced—usually between $50 and $75.

# Ingredients

All the ingredients used in the recipes in this book are easily accessible in most grocery stores throughout the country.

**Alcohol:** Stock your pantry with good-quality drinking liqueurs to flavor your French desserts. Some of my favorites are: Grand Marnier, dark rum (I like Meyers's brand), Cognac, Kahlúa, kirsch, Calvados, Poire William, and whiskey.

**Butter:** Unsalted butter is fresher tasting, and unsalted butter gives you better control over the salt content in your recipes.

**Chocolate:** There is a wide variation in the quality and cost of semisweet chocolate. The European brands Valrhona, Lindt, and Callebaut, and the American brand Scharffen Berger are highly regarded by chefs, but they are expensive and take extra effort for most people to find. I tested the recipes in this book with Nestlé semisweet chocolate morsels and Guittard semisweet chocolate morsels. They are widely available and their quality is good. If you are new to baking, start with these chocolates; they are more economical and you will be happy with the results. As you become more confident with these recipes and start branching out, try the more expensive chocolates—their flavor is incredible and will greatly enhance your desserts. My main goal is for you to try a new dessert or technique with ingredients that are easily accessible and not intimidating.

**Cocoa powder:** There are two types of unsweetened cocoa powder. Dutch-processed cocoa powder is the favorite of European bakers. Processed with alkali, it is less acidic, richer, and darker in color than natural cocoa powder. Droste is the most widely available brand of Dutch-processed cocoa powder. In French desserts that are briefly baked, that don't contain a lot of sugar or any chemical leavening agents like baking soda, or where cocoa is actually sprinkled on the dessert, the mellow flavor of Dutch-processed cocoa is the best choice. Natural cocoa powder, popular in American baking, is paler in color and very bitter on the tongue. Hershey's is a popular brand. Natural cocoa is the best choice in old-fashioned American cakes, brownies, and other desserts that have a high sugar content and are leavened with baking soda.

**Coffee:** I use French roast or Italian roast coffee beans. Store beans in the freezer and grind them right before you are ready to use them. Instant coffee or espresso powder can be used to create strong coffee extracts. Make sure the instant coffee you purchase has no added sweeteners or flavorings in it.

**Cream:** Most of the heavy cream in the dairy section of grocery stores today is ultra-pasteurized for a long shelf life. Although this is not ideal, searching out fresher, less processed cream can be difficult. If at all possible, use pasteurized cream with no additives like carrageenan or pectin, which is added to make the texture of cream seem thicker. Check the ingredient list on the back of the container and choose the brand with the fewest additives.

**Eggs:** Use large eggs for accurate results with these recipes. Large eggs weigh 2 ounces each, so weigh your eggs first for very accurate results.

**Extracts:** Always use extracts labeled "pure." Never use imitation vanilla or almond extracts, as their flavor can be bland or have a chemical aftertaste.

**Flour:** I tested the recipes in this book with the national brands Pillsbury and Gold Medal. Southern brands, like White Lily, tend to be softer, and the amount of flour would need to be adjusted. For accuracy, I used the brands most available across the country.

Unbleached all-purpose flour is a strong flour with a higher concentration of protein. Use unbleached all-purpose flour in all pâte à choux batters. Bleaching enhances the ability of flour to absorb moisture. Not quite as strong as unbleached flour, but not as soft as cake flour, bleached flour is perfect for sablé cookies, where you want a flour strong enough to support the ingredients but soft enough to create a tender dough. Cake flour is made from a softer wheat, is bleached, and is more finely milled than all-purpose flour. Essential for fine-textured, tender cakes, it is available in 2-pound boxes in most grocery stores under the brand names Softasilk and Swan's Down.

**Fruit:** For berry sauces and coulis, frozen unsweetened berries are actually a better choice than fresh. The fruit is very ripe when frozen, and the freezing process breaks down the fiber in the fruit, eliminating the need to cook the berries. The resulting puree is very smooth and intense, with a fresh berry flavor. For glazes and fillings, buy apricot, sour cherry, and raspberry preserves.

**Milk:** Whole milk was used exclusively in testing the recipes in this book, but low-fat milk can usually be substituted, with only a small difference in richness and texture.

**Sugar:** I tested recipes in this book using many different brands of standard granulated sugar. Different brands of granulated sugar can vary widely in the size of the sugar crystals—from very fine to very coarse. When the size of the sugar crystals is unimportant, I use granulated sugar. If sugar with a very fine grain is desirable, I use superfine sugar, which dissolves easily and blends thoroughly, with no trace of grittiness. Superfine sugar works especially well in custards and meringues. It is available in one-pound boxes in the baking aisle of most grocery stores. You can make your own superfine sugar by processing ordinary granulated sugar, after measuring, in a food processor for several seconds. Confectioners', or powdered, sugar is granulated sugar processed with cornstarch. It is used for sweet pastry dough, some meringues, and for dusting over desserts.

**Vanilla beans:** Long, thin, moist black pods filled with aromatic sticky black seeds. Derived from a tropical climbing orchid, vanilla beans are an invaluable ingredient in desserts. The tiny black seeds speckle homemade vanilla ice cream, crème brûlée, and crème anglaise, delivering an intense vanilla flavor. Make sure the pods are moist and fragrant. They are available in grocery stores, kitchenware shops, and spice shops.

# Cookies, Tea Cakes, and Pastries

# 1

IN AMERICA, PETITS FOURS ARE USUALLY SMALL CAKES glazed with pastel-colored fondant icing. In France, *petits fours* refers to a beguiling assortment of tiny cookies, tea cakes, and pastries available in most pâtisseries, created to tempt when a larger cake or tart is just too much. Even the most jaded appetite will have a difficult time refusing one of these charming treats. Just one or two mouthfuls, a buttery sablé, rich macaroon, airy meringue, crisp tuile, or tender madeleine is irresistible. Perfect sampled alone, with a steaming *café crème,* or nibbled alongside spoonfuls of a rich pot de crème or swirl of chocolate mousse, these small sweets are simple to prepare and a delight to eat.

**Sablé, which means "sandy" in French,** is the perfect description for these tender, buttery cookies. Similar to shortbread, but more delicate and crumbly, sablés are really just simple icebox cookies you slice and bake.

# *Vanilla Sablés* Makes about 2 dozen cookies

1 cup (2 sticks) unsalted butter, softened

¾ cup superfine sugar

1 large egg

1 tablespoon pure vanilla extract

2 cups bleached all-purpose flour

⅛ teaspoon salt

1. Combine the butter and the sugar in a large bowl. With an electric mixer set at medium-low speed, beat the butter and sugar together until the mixture is creamy and the grains of sugar are barely visible, 2 to 3 minutes.

2. Add the egg and vanilla and beat until the mixture is smooth and combined.

3. Sift the flour and salt into the butter mixture. Using a large wooden spoon, stir the flour into the butter until incorporated. (Mixing the flour in by hand instead of using the electric mixer avoids overworking the dough, which would make the cookies hard and tough.)

4. Divide the dough in half. On a sheet of waxed paper, form each half into a 10-inch log, using the paper to help form a smooth cylinder. Wrap tightly in the waxed paper and refrigerate for at least 2 hours or up to 1 week. For longer storage, wrap the logs a second time in plastic wrap and freeze for up to 1 month.

5. Place an oven rack on the middle shelf of the oven. Preheat the oven to 325°F. Line a baking sheet with parchment paper.

6. Using a long, sharp knife, slice the dough into ½-inch-thick rounds and place them on the prepared pan. Bake for 12 to 15 minutes, or until the edges of the cookies are a pale, golden brown but the centers of the cookies are still very pale. Remove the cookies from the baking sheet with a large metal spatula and let cool completely on a wire rack.

7. Store sablés in a tightly covered container for 2 to 3 days.

Vanilla Sablés with Chocolate-Hazelnut Sablés, *page 18*

*VARIATIONS:*

### Chocolate-Hazelnut Sablés

Follow the recipe for Vanilla Sablés (page 16), using 1$\frac{3}{4}$ cups flour and $\frac{1}{3}$ cup unsweetened Dutch-processed cocoa powder instead of 2 cups flour. Fold 1 cup whole skinned toasted hazelnuts (see page 19) into the dough. Chill, slice, and bake for 12 to 15 minutes, or until the cookies are firm and have a dull rather than shiny appearance.

### Dried Apricot and Candied-Almond Sablés

Follow the recipe for Vanilla Sablés (page 16), but use only $\frac{1}{2}$ cup superfine sugar. Gently knead $\frac{1}{2}$ cup crushed praline (page 136) and 1 cup diced dried apricots into the dough before chilling, slicing, and baking.

### Pistachio-Orange Sablés

Follow the recipe for Vanilla Sablés (page 16), adding the grated zest of 2 oranges with the egg and substituting 1 tablespoon Grand Marnier and 1 teaspoon pure orange extract for the vanilla extract. Fold 1 cup skinned toasted pistachios (see page 19) into the dough before chilling, slicing, and baking.

## TOASTING AND SKINNING NUTS

Often, recipes call for toasted nuts, as toasting enhances their full flavor. Walnuts, pecans, and blanched almonds taste even more delicious after they have been briefly toasted. Pistachios, raw almonds, and hazelnuts—the nuts with the most tenacious, papery skins—are usually skinned or blanched, since the color of the skin and its slightly bitter taste often interfere with the flavor and appearance of a dish.

**Toasting nuts to enhance flavor:** Preheat the oven to 350°F. Place the nuts in a single layer on a sided baking sheet. Bake for 5 to 8 minutes, until they are warm and fragrant, stirring the nuts several times and watching to make sure they don't burn. Remove the nuts from the oven and allow them to cool completely before chopping or grinding.

**Toasting and skinning hazelnuts and pistachios:** These nuts are toasted before skinning, both to heighten their flavor and to help loosen their slightly bitter skin. Preheat the oven to 350°F. Place the shelled nuts in a single layer on a sided baking sheet. Bake for 8 to 10 minutes, stirring the nuts several times and watching to make sure they don't burn. Immediately transfer the nuts to a clean kitchen towel. Rub them together vigorously in the towel to loosen and remove the skins. Don't worry if some of the skins remain; the unique flavor of the nuts will not be compromised.

**Blanching and skinning almonds:** Bring 2 or 3 cups of water to a boil. Stir in up to 1 cup of shelled almonds and remove the pan from heat. Allow the nuts to sit in the hot water for 2 to 3 minutes. Drain and let cool to the touch. You should now be able to peel the skins from the nuts easily with your fingers. Sometimes soaking almonds in water can soften them; if this happens, toast the dried, skinned almonds in a preheated 350°F oven for about 2 minutes to restore their crunchy texture. Watch carefully and do not let them brown.

**There is a reason classic recipes endure.** These crisp, roof tile–shaped cookies are quick to put together, and they are versatile, delicious treats to serve with ice cream, pots de crème, or fresh fruit.

# *Almond Tuiles* Makes 3 dozen cookies

3 large egg whites

1 1/4 cups confectioners' sugar, sifted

1/2 cup all-purpose unbleached flour

Pinch of salt

5 tablespoons unsalted butter, melted

1 teaspoon pure vanilla extract

1/8 teaspoon pure almond extract

1 1/4 cups sliced almonds

1. Place an oven rack on the middle shelf of the oven. Preheat the oven to 375°F. Line a baking sheet with parchment paper.

2. Combine the egg whites, confectioners' sugar, flour, and salt in a medium bowl and whisk until smooth. Stir in the melted butter, vanilla and almond extract, and almonds.

3. Spoon level tablespoonfuls of the batter onto the prepared pan at least 3 inches apart. Using a small metal icing spatula or the back of a fork, spread the batter as thinly as possible into a 2- or 3-inch circle. If the sliced almonds stick or clump together, gently separate them with the tines of the fork.

4. Bake the cookies for 7 to 9 minutes, or until the edges are golden brown but

the centers are still pale. Remove the cookies from the oven, and while they are still warm and flexible, remove them from the baking sheet with a metal spatula and gently lay each one over a rolling pin to cool. To shape into cigarettes, cones, or bowls, see Shaping Tuiles (page 22).

5. Store cookies in a tightly covered container for up to 2 to 3 days.

**Fresh rosemary may seem like an unusual addition to a delicate, lacy cookie,** but at the restaurant Campagne et Provence in Paris, the chef shapes tuiles infused with this intense herb into tall, thin triangles and serves them propped up against an airy mound of orange-scented chocolate mousse. The result is a surprisingly delicious and vibrant combination of flavors reminiscent of the French countryside.

# ROSEMARY-ALMOND TUILES   Makes 3½ to 4 dozen cookies

⅔ cup sugar

½ cup (1 stick) unsalted butter, softened

⅓ cup light corn syrup

1 cup cake flour, sifted

1 cup finely chopped almonds

2 tablespoons minced fresh rosemary

1. Place an oven rack on the middle shelf of the oven. Preheat the oven to 325°F. Line a baking sheet with parchment paper.

2. In a medium bowl, stir the sugar and butter together with a wooden spoon until smooth and creamy. Stir the corn syrup into the butter mixture.

3. Stir the flour, almonds, and rosemary into the batter.

4. Place level tablespoonfuls of batter at least 2 inches apart on the prepared pan. Bake for 7 to 10 minutes, or until the batter has spread into thin, lacy cookies and is golden brown.

5. Remove the baking sheet from the oven and let the cookies cool completely on the parchment paper, then remove with an offset spatula. Or, to shape into tuiles, cones, or cigarettes, see Shaping Tuiles (page 22). The cookies will become very crisp as they cool.

6. Store tuiles in a tightly covered container for up to 2 to 3 days.

## SHAPING TUILES

After you remove the baking sheet from the oven, let the cookies "set" for a few seconds before removing them from the baking sheet. Should any of the cookies grow too brittle as you are shaping them, return them to the hot oven for a few seconds to soften.

**Tuile:** To form this classic, gently curving roof-tile shape, remove the warm cookies from the baking sheet with a large metal spatula and lay each cookie over a rolling pin to cool.

**Cigarettes:** Place one end of a warm cookie against the handle of a wooden spoon and very quickly roll the cookie over itself into a tight tube shape. If the bowl of the spoon gets in the way of swift rolling, go ahead and sacrifice an inexpensive wooden spoon and lop off its head, using a small saw to do so.

Alternatively, you can purchase a small length of dowel at the hardware store. Most hardware stores will cut the length of dowel that you want; a 6-inch-long dowel that is $^3/_8$ inch to $^1/_2$ inch in diameter works well.

**Cones:** Kitchenware stores carry small wooden cones with a handle, specifically created to shape flexible lace cookies into cones. Wrap a warm cookie around the cone and allow it to cool. Cones can be shaped by hand as well; holding both sides of a cookie, wrap one side over the

other, forming a point at one end and a larger opening at the other. You can create a charming dessert using cookie cones by placing 3 on a dessert plate and filling each with a different flavor ice cream or mousse.

**Bowls:** To form a cookie bowl to hold mousse, ice cream, or fresh fruit, lay a warm cookie over the bottom of a small custard cup turned upside down. Use your fingers to gently mold the cookie to the contours of the bowl as it cools.

# GRATING CITRUS ZEST

Zest is the brightly colored and scented outer rind of citrus fruit. The zest of oranges, lemons, and limes contains all the aromatic essential oils, and it packs a huge punch of citrus flavor essential for cooking.

You can grate the zest by scraping the fruit against the smallest holes of a box grater. Do not grate into the white skin, or "pith," of the orange, as it is very bitter. Using this method produces a very fine, soft, almost juicy zest that dissolves beautifully, but it is sometimes difficult to remove from the grater. Remove the zest from behind the sharp holes with the back of a blunt knife.

Use a small, clean children's toothbrush (reserved for this purpose only) to brush any remaining bits of zest from around the sharp holes onto a small plate or piece of waxed paper.

You can also use a small tool called, conveniently, a zester. A zester has a small head with four or five sharp holes that quickly shred the zest from the fruit in long, thin ribbons when you pull it down the outside of the fruit. Using a zester also guarantees that you will remove all the flavorful zest and none of the bitter white pith beneath it. The ribbons of zest can be finely chopped or, if you are using the zest in a recipe containing sugar, you can pulverize the zest together with the sugar in a blender or food processor.

**Florentines are enduring favorites in most French pastry shops.** Heating the butter, sugar, and corn syrup together before stirring in the remaining ingredients produces a very sturdy, beautifully glossy cookie with a faint caramel flavor.

# *Chocolate Florentines*  Makes 2 to 3 dozen cookies

⅔ cup sugar

½ cup (1 stick) unsalted butter

⅓ cup light corn syrup

1 cup sliced almonds

¼ cup diced candied
orange peel (optional)

1 cup cake flour, sifted

Pinch of salt

1 cup semisweet chocolate
morsels

1. In a medium, heavy saucepan, combine the sugar, butter, and corn syrup. Stir constantly over medium heat until the butter is melted and the mixture is smooth and combined.

2. Bring the mixture to a boil. Remove the pan from heat and stir in the almonds and candied orange peel, if using. Add the flour and salt to the batter and stir until smooth. Transfer the batter to a cool metal bowl to speed up the cooling time. Let the batter chill for at least 1 hour. At this point the batter can be covered and refrigerated for up to 1 week. The batter will be very stiff.

3. Place an oven rack on the middle shelf of the oven. Preheat the oven to 325°F. Line a baking sheet with parchment paper.

4. Roll level tablespoonfuls of batter between your palms into small balls. Place them on the prepared pan at least 3 inches apart.

5. Bake the florentines for 7 to 10 minutes, until they are flat, lacy, and a deep golden brown. Remove the pan from the oven and allow the florentines to cool completely on the pan on a wire rack.

6. Melt the chocolate in a double boiler over barely simmering water, stirring constantly, or in a microwave oven.

7. Use a metal spatula to remove a cooled florentine from the baking sheet. Spread 1 or 2 teaspoons melted chocolate over the bottom of each florentine. Give the florentine a decorative flourish by tracing a wavy pattern of lines across the soft chocolate, using the tines of a fork. Alternatively, you can sandwich 2 florentines together with melted chocolate in the middle.

8. Store florentines in a tightly covered container for up to 2 to 3 days.

Chocolate Florentines

# MELTING CHOCOLATE

Melting chocolate requires gentle heat. If melted at too high a heat it may scorch, burn and become hard and granular instead of velvety smooth.

## CHOCOLATE CAN BE MELTED IN TWO WAYS:

**Stovetop:** Place coarsely chopped chocolate or chocolate morsels in the top of a double boiler over barely simmering water. Stir constantly until the chocolate is melted and smooth. Do not let the water boil; boiling creates steam, and the condensation from the steam, if it comes into contact with the chocolate, will make it "seize," or become coarse and grainy.

**Microwave:** Place coarsely chopped chocolate or chocolate morsels in a microwave-safe bowl and microwave for $1^{1}/_{2}$ to 4 minutes, or until the chocolate softens and becomes shiny but still retains its shape. Remove the bowl from the microwave and stir the chocolate until it is completely melted and smooth. If melting milk or white chocolate, stir after $1^{1}/_{2}$ minutes. Both of these chocolates melt faster and scorch easier than semisweet or bittersweet chocolate.

**Parisian pâtisserie windows are amassed with clouds of meringues:** snowy white or tinted in pastel shades of pink or green, some sprinkled with almonds or sandwiched with cream. These crisp, sweet ephemera are a snap to prepare if you follow a few simple techniques. Egg whites and sugar are beaten together until they form stiff, glossy "peaks," which guarantees that the batter will not lose its shape when piped or spooned onto a baking sheet. Be sure to prepare your meringues on a very dry day–humidity plays havoc with the crisp meringue. Sugar absorbs moisture from the atmosphere, and your crisp, airy meringues will turn into soggy, sugary lumps. The perfect meringue is a pristine, snowy white and thoroughly crisp and dry. Reduce the oven temperature if you notice your meringues beginning to color, or prop the oven door open slightly with the handle of a wooden spoon to release any excess heat and steam.

# FRENCH MERINGUES   Makes 2 dozen 4-inch meringues

| | | |
|---|---|---|
| 6 egg whites at room temperature | Pinch of salt | 1 teaspoon pure vanilla extract |
| ½ teaspoon cream of tartar | 1 cup superfine sugar | 1 cup confectioners' sugar, sifted |

1. Place 1 oven rack on the middle shelf of the oven and place a second rack on the top shelf. Preheat the oven to 200°F. Line 2 baking sheets with parchment paper.

2. In a large bowl, beat the egg whites and cream of tartar with an electric mixer at low speed until foamy. Add the salt and increase the mixer speed to medium high and continue beating until soft peaks form. Continue beating, adding the superfine sugar 1 tablespoon at a time until stiff, glossy peaks form. Beat in the vanilla.

3. Sift the confectioners' sugar, a second time, over the meringue. Using a rubber spatula, carefully fold the sugar into the meringue just until no streaks of sugar remain. Do not fold any more than is necessary, as overmixing will deflate the meringue. You want the mixture to hold stiff peaks, which ensures that the meringues hold their shape.

4. Use a large serving spoon to scoop twelve ¼-cup portions of the meringue mixture onto each of the prepared pans. Do not take too much care forming the meringues—they should be free-form, cloudlike confections.

5. Bake the meringues for 2 hours, or until crisp. Baking the meringues for a long period of time at a very low temperature assures that they will remain very white and become quite crisp. If the oven seems too hot, or the meringues are beginning to color, reduce the heat to 175°F and prop the oven door open slightly with the handle of a wooden spoon. When the meringues are crisp, turn the oven off and let the meringues cool in the oven for 1 to 6 hours.

6. Store the cooled meringues in a tightly covered container for up to 1 week.

# MASTERING MERINGUE

Three types of meringue are traditionally used in French desserts: French, Swiss, and Italian. Each is prepared in a slightly different way, which makes them ideally suited for specific desserts.

**French meringue:** The simplest and quickest to prepare, but the most fragile of the meringues. Egg whites are beaten to soft peaks, granulated sugar is added gradually, and the mixture is beaten until the meringue forms stiff, glossy peaks that hold their shape without drooping when a portion of meringue is scooped up with the whisk or beaters. Confectioners' sugar is then folded in by hand, and the meringue is piped into various shapes or simply spooned onto a baking sheet in cloudlike formations. French meringue is always baked, and it must be baked as soon as it is made—it will collapse and separate if allowed to sit too long. French meringue is crisp and delicate and the best choice for plain meringue cookies.

**Swiss meringue:** A sturdier, less delicate form of meringue. With a good free-standing mixer, this former bad boy of the meringue world becomes the easiest to master of the three described here. Egg whites and confectioners' or granulated sugar are beaten together in a metal bowl set over simmering water until the sugar is dissolved and the mixture is very hot—about 120°F. It is then removed from the heat and beaten until thick, fluffy, glossy, and completely cool. With a free-standing mixer, the herculean effort required to beat the meringue until cool is a snap. There is little danger of overbeating this meringue, and it does not require the precision or timing that Italian meringue demands. Swiss meringue is less delicate than French meringue and can be—but doesn't have to be—cooked a second time. Because it is a denser, less delicate meringue, Swiss meringue makes wonderful meringue shells and boxes that, when baked, are very crunchy and hold up well to wet fillings such as ice creams or mousses, and it stays crisper longer when covered with a fruit or chocolate sauce. Swiss meringue is a wonderful base for buttercream and can be stored for long periods of time without separating or collapsing.

**Italian meringue:** More difficult to master, but supremely versatile, this meringue is very sturdy, with a wonderfully silky texture. Italian meringue is prepared by drizzling a hot sugar syrup into well-beaten egg whites to form a meringue that is smooth, silky, and almost indestructible. It can sit for hours or be refrigerated for days without collapsing. It is the most commonly used base for French buttercream, and it can be folded into pastry cream to lighten and sweeten it or used as a base for frozen soufflés. Italian meringue can also be baked into cookies, although the texture will be more fragile and delicate than that of French or Swiss meringue.

# BEATING EGG WHITES

The task of beating egg whites into a stable foam to fold into soufflés and cakes or to create meringue buttercreams or meringue cookies is simplified by following these simple instructions.

1. **Separate cold eggs:** Eggs separate easily and cleanly when they are cold. For greater volume, let egg whites come to room temperature before beating.

2. **Keep whites fat-free:** Egg whites must be free from any traces of yolk or other grease or oils to whip up properly. Any traces of fat will destroy the egg white's ability to trap and hold air. If you notice a touch of egg yolk in the separated whites, remove it with one of the empty egg shells; the yolk is attracted to the shell and will be easier to remove.

3. **Use cream of tartar:** Adding cream of tartar to the egg whites as you beat them will ensure that they develop a dense, creamy foam with maximum volume that is more stable and less likely to collapse. Beating egg whites in a copper bowl performs the same function that cream of tartar does.

4. **Use a metal bowl:** In the absence of a copper bowl, use a large stainless steel bowl. It is difficult to keep plastic bowls free from all traces of oil or fat, and the smooth sides of glass or ceramic bowls make it hard for the whites to cling together and form a close, tight structure.

5. **Start slowly for stability:** To create a more stable egg white foam with fewer chances of collapsing, start beating whites at low speed, then increase the speed to medium when the whites are no longer viscous and start to foam. Starting at a low speed will develop smaller bubbles in the foam. These are inherently more stable than large bubbles, which would form if you started beating the egg whites at high speed.

6. **Don't overbeat:** After the egg whites have achieved stiff, glossy peaks, stop beating. Overbeating causes the whites to separate and become dry and granular, eventually collapsing.

7. **Beat to soft peaks:** Soft peaks are formed when the egg whites develop soft, billowy mounds with well-defined peaks that slowly curve when the beaters are lifted. The beaten whites will not cling to the sides of the bowl, but shift from side to side in one mass when the bowl is tilted. Egg whites beaten to the soft-peak stage are the perfect consistency for folding into soufflés, mousses, and cake batters. They are firm enough to hold their shape without deflating, but incorporate easily with other ingredients. Egg whites beaten to soft peaks will continue to expand in the oven when they are baked, ensuring high-rising soufflés and cakes.

8. **Beat to stiff, glossy peaks:** Egg whites beaten to stiff, glossy peaks will have a dense, creamy texture and stand firmly upright when the beaters are lifted. Egg whites beaten to stiff peaks are so smooth and firm that they will not fall out of the bowl if it is turned upside down. Until you can "eyeball" stiff peaks, feel free to stop the mixer and check how firmly the peaks stand up when the beaters are lifted. Egg whites beaten to stiff peaks are very firm and hold their shape well, making them perfect for meringue cookies, baskets, and decorations.

**These cookies are a sublime combination** of crisp white meringue concealing a heart of dark, creamy chocolate ganache. Both the meringues and the ganache can be made up to 1 week in advance, but don't combine the two until the day you are ready to serve them.

# *Moor's Kisses*   Makes about 2½ dozen cookies

**French Meringue batter (page 27)**   **1 cup semisweet chocolate morsels**   **½ cup chocolate jimmies**
**Chocolate Ganache (page 131)**                                                   **(sprinkles) for coating**

1. Place 1 oven rack on the middle shelf of the oven, and a second rack on the top shelf. Preheat the oven to 200°F. Line 2 baking sheets with parchment paper.

2. Fill a piping bag with the meringue. It isn't necessary to use a pastry tip. Squeeze large "kiss"-shaped meringues onto the prepared pans. Bake as in the French meringue recipe and let cool.

3. Holding a kiss in one hand, use the forefinger of your other hand to gently push into the bottom of the meringue, creating a hole inside the cookie.

4. Fit a piping bag with a ¼-inch (No. 2) plain pastry tip and fill with the ganache. In a pinch, you can fashion a "faux" piping bag by filling a self-sealing plastic bag with ganache, cutting off the tip from one corner of the bag. Squeeze the ganache into the hollowed meringue, filling it. Repeat to fill the remaining meringues.

5. In a double boiler over barely simmering water, stir the chocolate morsels until melted. Or, place the chocolate morsels in a microwave-safe bowl and microwave for 1½ to 4 minutes, or until the chocolate softens and becomes shiny but still maintains its

shape. Remove the bowl from the microwave and stir the chocolate until it is completely melted and smooth.

6. Fill a small bowl with the chocolate jimmies. Line a baking sheet with waxed paper or parchment paper. Dip the base of each cookie in the melted chocolate and immediately dip in the chocolate jimmies. Place the kisses on the paper-lined pan. Let the kisses sit until the chocolate hardens. Store meringues in a tightly covered container in a cool place. Do not refrigerate, or the meringue will soften. Serve within 24 hours.

Moor's Kisses

If I were a poet, nothing less than a love sonnet would do to illuminate the subtle allure of the French macaroon. These creamy, glossy, ecru rounds of almond meringue have delicately thin, crisp shells concealing a creamy, chewy interior. The reputations of Parisian pastry chefs are won and lost on the basis of the perfect macaroon. Pastry chefs all over Paris flavor these popular macaroons with pistachio, coffee, chocolate, lemon, and raspberry, tinting them in a rainbow of colors to match their flavors. Queen-sized macaroons line up aristocratically in pâtisserie windows next to tiny silver dollar–sized babies called *gerbets*. Macaroons are no more difficult to master than meringues, and given the ecstatic moments they inspire in many people, they are well worth the effort.

# *A*LMOND *M*ACAROONS

Makes 20 sandwiched 1-inch macaroons

1½ cups (6 ounces) slivered blanched almonds

2 cups confectioners' sugar

3 egg whites at room temperature

⅛ teaspoon cream of tartar

3 tablespoons granulated sugar

Pinch of salt

½ teaspoon pure vanilla extract

⅛ teaspoon pure almond extract

Almond Butter Filling (page 34) or Chocolate Ganache (page 131)

1. Place an oven rack on the top shelf of the oven. Preheat the oven to 450°F. Line 2 baking sheets with parchment paper.

2. Combine the almonds and confectioners' sugar in a food processor. Pulse together until the mixture is very fine and powdery.

3. In a large bowl, combine the egg whites and cream of tartar. Using an electric mixer set at medium-low speed, beat the egg whites until soft peaks form. Continue beating, adding the granulated sugar 1 tablespoon at a time, until stiff, glossy peaks form.

4. With a large rubber spatula, gently fold the almond mixture, salt, and vanilla and almond extracts into the meringue. It will deflate slightly after the sugar and almonds are folded in, but the batter should not be so loose or runny that it can't be piped into mounds and hold its shape.

5. Fill a large 16-inch or 18-inch piping bag with the macaroon mixture—there is no need to fit the bag with a tip, as the bag's opening is just the right size for piping the macaroons. Pipe 1-inch mounds of the batter onto the prepared pans.

6. Let the macaroons sit for 20 minutes. This allows a crust to form; as the macaroons bake, they will extrude a circular rim of meringue that forms a base, called "the foot," the hallmark of properly baked macaroons that gives them their distinctive appearance.

RECIPE CONTINUES >>

Almond Macaroons

7. Bake the macaroons (1 sheet at a time) for 1 minute. Reduce the oven temperature to 375°F and slip a second, unlined baking sheet underneath the sheet of macaroons. This will preserve the macaroons' delicate beige color and keep them from browning too much. Bake for 8 to 10 minutes, or until the macaroons have a smooth, shiny surface and are dry to the touch.

8. Lift the first baking sheet off the second and remove it from the oven and place it on a wire rack. Lift one corner of the parchment up and pour about ¼ cup cold water directly on the hot baking sheet under the parchment. Tilt the baking sheet so the water runs *under* the parchment over the entire surface of the baking sheet (without getting the macaroons wet, of course). The steam from the water will release the macaroons from the parchment paper. Let the cookies cool on the paper for a few minutes before carefully removing them to a wire cooling rack with a metal spatula.

9. Spread 1 or 2 teaspoons of the almond butter filling or chocolate ganache on the bottom of one macaroon with a small metal icing spatula. Press a second cookie on top of the filling to form a sandwich. Repeat to fill the remaining macaroons. For a lighter version of the cookie, sandwich 2 macaroons together without any filling as soon as you remove them from the baking sheet, while the bottoms of the cookies are still damp enough to stick together.

**VARIATION: *Chocolate Ganache Macaroons***

Sift 3 tablespoons Dutch-processed cocoa powder and add to the ground almond mixture in the food processor in step 2 of Almond Macaroon recipe. Pulse a few times to combine. Proceed with the recipe, deleting the almond extract. Sandwich the macaroons using Chocolate Ganache (page 131).

# ALMOND BUTTER FILLING Makes about ⅓ cup

**3 tablespoons unsalted butter, softened**

**3½ ounces almond paste**

**¼ teaspoon pure vanilla extract**

Combine all the ingredients in a food processor and process until smooth and creamy. Or, combine all the ingredients in a medium bowl, and beat together using an electric mixer set at medium-low speed, until creamy.

**Madeleines are traditionally flavored with lemon.** Ground almonds and browned butter give these added richness.

# Lemon-Almond Madeleines  Makes about 2 dozen madeleines

2 large eggs

2 egg whites

⅓ cup granulated sugar

2 tablespoons fresh lemon juice

Grated zest of 1 lemon

1 teaspoon pure vanilla extract or lemon extract

½ cup slivered blanched almonds

1 cup confectioners' sugar

¾ cup unbleached all-purpose flour

Pinch of salt

¾ cup (1½ sticks) unsalted butter, browned (see page 38)

1. Using a large wire whisk, gently beat the eggs, egg whites, granulated sugar, lemon juice, lemon zest, and vanilla or lemon extract together in a large bowl just until combined.

2. Combine the almonds and confectioners' sugar in a food processor and grind until fine and powdery. Sift together the flour and salt and fold into the batter with the almond mixture. Gently stir the browned butter into the batter. The batter will be fairly thin. Cover the bowl with plastic wrap and refrigerate for at least 1 hour or up to 24 hours. After chilling, the batter will be thick and firm.

3. Place an oven rack on the middle shelf of the oven. Preheat the oven to 375°F. Spray the molds of a madeleine pan with nonstick vegetable-oil cooking spray. Fill each shell mold with 1 tablespoon batter. Place the madeleine pan on a baking sheet and bake the madeleines for 10 to 12 minutes, or until they are firm, the edges are golden brown and they develop a small hump in the center.

4. Remove the madeleines from the pan, popping them out of their molds with the tip of a paring knife. Let cool on a wire rack. Wipe any stray crumbs from the madeleine pan with a paper towel, spray again with nonstick vegetable-oil cooking spray and repeat to bake the remaining batter.

5. Madeleines are at their best eaten the day they are baked, but they can be tightly wrapped and frozen for up to 1 week.

Honey Madeleines

**These seductive little seashell-shaped cakes** may not unlock a torrent of memories for you as they did for Proust, but their innate romance is sure to beguile you. I should know; years ago, in a misguided fit of entrepreneurial verve, I purchased about three dozen madeleine pans, intent on providing every caterer in San Diego with these dainty little cakes. Although my brush with big business was mercifully brief, I'm still in love with madeleines. I made dozens of them, along with dolphin-shaped sablés, for my daughter's Hawaiian-themed fifth birthday party. They were a huge hit with the kindergarten set. The browned butter, or *beurre noisette*, in the batter, gives these little cakes a speckled crumb; a moist, rich interior; and a faintly nutty flavor.

# HONEY MADELEINES    Makes about 2 dozen madeleines

2 large eggs

2 egg whites

⅓ cup granulated sugar

1 teaspoon pure vanilla extract

2 tablespoons honey

1 cup unbleached all-purpose
  flour

1 cup confectioners' sugar

Pinch of salt

¾ cup (1½ sticks) unsalted
  butter, browned (see page 38)

1. Using a large wire whisk, gently beat the eggs, egg whites, granulated sugar, vanilla, and honey together in a large bowl just until combined.

2. Sift the flour, confectioners' sugar, and salt together and fold into the batter. Gently fold the browned butter into the batter until completely smooth. The batter will be fairly thin. Cover the bowl with plastic wrap and refrigerate for at least 1 hour or up to 24 hours. After chilling, the batter will be thick and firm.

3. Place an oven rack on the middle shelf of the oven. Preheat the oven to 375°F. Spray the molds of a madeleine pan with nonstick vegetable-oil cooking spray. Fill each shell mold with 1 tablespoon batter. Place the pan on a baking sheet and bake for 10 to 12 minutes, or until the madeleines are firm and golden brown with a small hump in the center.

4. Remove the madeleines from the pan, popping them out with the tip of a paring knife. Let cool on a wire rack. Wipe any stray crumbs from the pan with a paper towel, spray again with nonstick vegetable-oil cooking spray, and repeat to bake the remaining batter.

5. Madeleines are at their best eaten the day they are baked, but they can be tightly wrapped and frozen for up to 1 week.

### VARIATION: *Coconut Madeleines*

Follow the above recipe for Honey Madeleines, but eliminate the honey and instead stir 1 cup shredded coconut into the batter after the browned butter has been incorporated, at the end of step 2.

# BROWNED BUTTER

When butter is melted and cooked until it begins to turn brown, it develops a sweet, slightly nutty flavor as the milk solids in the butter start to caramelize. This delicious browned butter, or *beurre noisette,* which literally means "nut butter," is a delicious addition to many French dishes, including many tea cakes and other desserts.

**To make browned butter:** Melt unsalted butter in a medium saucepan over low heat. Increase heat and bring the butter to a boil. Continue cooking, stirring constantly, until the solids at the bottom of the pan begin to brown. As the milk solids begin to caramelize, the butter will develop the sweet, slightly nutty aroma of *beurre noisette;* this should take about 5 minutes. Immediately strain the butter into a heatproof bowl to cool and prevent the butter from browning any further in the hot pan. Let cool completely.

# HOW THE MADELEINE GOT ITS HUMP AND OTHER HELPFUL HINTS

In order for the madeleines to achieve the distinctive humped back they are famous for, the eggs must not be beaten excessively and the batter must be refrigerated until the melted butter solidifies and the batter becomes very firm and cold. Baked at high heat, some of the cold batter spreads out to fill the mold and the center bakes into the characteristic hump.

Make sure you use classic metal madeleine pans; the traditional pan yields madeleines with sharp distinctive pleats. Avoid madeleine pans made from black steel and nonstick pans. The black pans make the madeleines brown too quickly, and nonstick pans don't form the distinctive pleats as clearly as the traditional pans do.

**Hazelnuts are a natural match with chocolate,** but you can substitute almonds or walnuts if you prefer.

# CHOCOLATE-HAZELNUT MADELEINES

### Makes about 2 dozen madeleines

2 large eggs

2 egg whites

⅓ cup granulated sugar

1 teaspoon pure vanilla extract

½ cup hazelnuts, toasted, skinned and finely chopped (see page 19)

1 cup confectioners' sugar

½ cup unbleached all-purpose flour

¼ cup unsweetened Dutch processed cocoa powder

Pinch of salt

¾ cup (1½ sticks) unsalted butter, melted and cooled

1. Using a large wire whisk, gently beat the eggs, egg whites, granulated sugar, and vanilla together in a large bowl just until combined.

2. Combine the hazelnuts and confectioners' sugar in a food processor and grind together until fine and powdery. Sift together the flour, cocoa powder, and salt and fold into the batter along with the hazelnut mixture. Stir the cooled melted butter gently into the batter. The batter will be fairly thin. Cover the bowl with plastic wrap and refrigerate for at least 1 hour or up to 24 hours. After chilling, the batter will be thick and firm.

3. Place an oven rack on the middle shelf of the oven. Preheat the oven to 375°F. Spray the molds of a madeleine pan with nonstick vegetable-oil cooking spray. Fill each shell mold with 1 tablespoon batter. Place the prepared pan on a baking sheet and bake the madeleines for 10 to 12 minutes, or until they are firm and develop a small hump in the center.

4. Remove the madeleines from the pan, popping them out of their molds with the tip of a paring knife. Let cool on a wire rack. Wipe any stray crumbs from the madeleine pan with a paper towel, spray again with vegetable-oil cooking spray, and repeat to bake the remaining batter

5. Madeleines are at their best eaten the day they are baked, but they can be tightly wrapped and frozen for up to 1 week.

## NUT FLOURS

Nut flour is merely nuts ground so fine they resemble a powdery flour. Used often in French pastry, almond and other nut "flours" are available commercially in Europe. Almond flour is difficult, if not impossible, to find in American supermarkets, but it can be simulated with the help of a food processor. To achieve the fine texture necessary for the madeleines and financiers in this book, grind the nuts with confectioners' sugar until they are very fine and powdery. It is necessary to grind the nuts with either sugar or flour. These ingredients act as a buffer; if ground alone, the nuts would turn into an oily paste before they were ground as fine as they need to be for these recipes.

**The last time I went to Paris,** it was partly in search of the perfect financier. The French pastry chef's "little black dress," these buttery cakes, shaped like small gold bricks, are sheer, simple perfection. According to Patricia Wells, author of *Bistro Cooking* and *The Food Lover's Guide to Paris,* the perfect financier has a "firm, crusty exterior, and a moist almondy interior, tasting almost as if they were filled with almond paste." This recipe, adapted from her own, heightens the almond flavor by browning the butter and adding a splash of dark rum. Financier pans made of tin or newer pans made from nonstick Silpat are available from most kitchen supply stores. You can also bake these in mini muffin pans or small tartlet pans; the flavor will be just as delicious.

# $\mathcal{F}$INANCIERS    Makes about 2 dozen cakes

1½ cups (6 ounces) slivered
   blanched almonds

1½ cups confectioners' sugar

¾ cup granulated sugar

9 egg whites

2 tablespoons dark rum, or
   1 teaspoon vanilla extract

½ teaspoon pure almond extract

¾ cup unbleached all-purpose flour

¼ teaspoon salt

1 cup (2 sticks) unsalted butter,
   browned (see page 38)

1. Combine the almonds and confectioners' sugar in a food processor. Grind the nuts and sugar together until fine and powdery.

2. Transfer the nut mixture to a large bowl and stir in the granulated sugar, egg whites, rum or vanilla, and almond extract just until smooth and combined. Sift the flour and salt together and gently fold into the batter.

3. Gently stir the browned butter into the batter. Cover the bowl with plastic wrap and refrigerate until the batter is very firm and cold, at least 1 hour or up to 24 hours.

4. Place an oven rack on the middle shelf of the oven. Preheat oven to 450°F.

5. Spray the molds of a financier pan, or the cups of a mini muffin pan, with nonstick vegetable-oil cooking spray. Either fill a piping bag with the financier batter or use a tablespoon to fill the prepared molds three-fourths full with batter. Place the financier pan on a baking sheet and bake for 7 minutes. Reduce the oven temperature to 400°F and bake for an additional 7 minutes. Remove the financiers from the oven, unmold, and let cool on a wire rack.

**I like to bake these financiers in a larger pan;** a muffin-top pan or small tartlet pans are perfect. They have a larger circumference but still retain the same chewy exterior and moist interior of their bite-sized cousins.

# HAZELNUT-RASPBERRY FINANCIERS   Makes 8 to 10 cakes

1½ cups (7 ounces) hazelnuts, toasted and skinned (page 19)

1½ cups confectioners' sugar, plus additional for dusting

¾ cup granulated sugar

9 egg whites

2 tablespoons hazelnut liqueur or Cognac

½ teaspoon pure vanilla extract

¾ cups unbleached all-purpose flour

¼ teaspoon salt

1 cup (2 sticks) unsalted butter, browned (see page 38)

80 (about 3 cups, loosely packed) unblemished fresh raspberries

Vanilla ice cream or Crème Chantilly (page 129) for serving

1. Combine the hazelnuts and confectioners' sugar in a food processor. Grind the nuts and sugar together until fine and powdery.

2. Transfer the nut mixture to a large bowl and stir in the granulated sugar, egg whites, hazelnut liqueur or Cognac, and vanilla extract just until smooth and combined. Sift the flour and salt together and gently fold into the batter.

3. Stir the browned butter into the batter. Cover the bowl with plastic wrap and refrigerate the batter until it is very firm and cold, at least 1 hour or up to 24 hours.

4. Place an oven rack on the middle shelf of the oven. Preheat the oven to 450°F. Spray eight 4¾-inch tartlet pans or muffin-top pans with nonstick vegetable-oil cooking spray. Fill three-fourths full with batter (about ⅓ cup batter).

5. Press 8 to 10 raspberries over the surface of each cake, rounded sides up. Place the pans on a baking sheet and bake for 10 minutes. Reduce the oven temperature to 400°F and bake for an additional 10 to 15 minutes, or until firm and golden brown. Remove the financiers from the oven, let cool briefly, and unmold.

6. Dust the financiers with confectioners' sugar and serve warm with a scoop of vanilla ice cream or a dollop of Crème Chantilly.

Hazelnut-Raspberry Financiers with Financiers, *page 41*

**Walnuts are softer and slightly oilier than almonds or hazelnuts,** so I have reduced the amount of butter in these financiers to compensate.

# Chocolate-Dipped Walnut Financiers

### Makes about 2 dozen cookies

1½ cups (7 ounces) chopped walnuts

1½ cups confectioners' sugar

¾ cup granulated sugar

9 egg whites

1½ teaspoons vanilla extract

¾ cup unbleached all-purpose flour

¼ teaspoon salt

¾ cup (1½ sticks) unsalted butter, browned (see page 38)

1 cup semisweet chocolate morsels

1 teaspoon vegetable shortening

1. Combine the walnuts and confectioner's sugar in a food processor. Grind the nuts and sugar together until fine and powdery.

2. Transfer the nut mixture to a mixing bowl and stir in the granulated sugar, egg whites, and vanilla extract just until smooth and combined. Sift flour and salt together and gently fold into the batter.

3. Gently stir in the browned butter. Cover the bowl with plastic wrap and refrigerate the batter until it is very firm and cold, at least 1 hour or up to 24 hours.

4. Place an oven rack on the middle shelf of the oven. Preheat the oven to 450°F. Spray the molds of a financier pan, or the cups of a mini muffin pan, with nonstick vegetable-oil cooking spray.

5. Either fill a piping bag with the financier batter or use a tablespoon to fill the prepared molds three-fourths full with batter. Place the financier pan on a baking sheet and bake for 7 minutes. Reduce the oven temperature to 400°F. and bake for an additional 7 minutes. Remove the financiers from the oven, unmold, and let cool on a wire rack.

6. In the top of a double boiler, over barely simmering water, melt semisweet chocolate morsels together with vegetable shortening. Stir until smooth. Or, combine the chocolate and the shortening in a microwave-safe bowl. Heat, uncovered, on medium power for 1½ to 4 minutes, or until the chocolate becomes soft and shiny but still maintains its shape. Remove the bowl from the microwave and stir the chocolate until it is completely melted and smooth.

7. Dip one end of each financier in the melted chocolate. Place on waxed paper or parchment paper until the chocolate hardens.

Cream puffs—crisp, pâte à choux pastries bulging with whipped cream—are my daughter's absolutely favorite dessert, and they are one of the most basic components of French pastry. Pâte à choux can be prepared with milk, water, or a combination of the two. For cream puffs, I like to make the pâte à choux with water alone. I think the filled pastry remains crisper longer. The pastry still has a slightly moist interior and the buttery, pleasantly eggy flavor which is the trademark of perfect pâte à choux. Make sure you bake pâte à choux on a standard baking sheet, and not an insulated one. Insulated baking sheets shield the pastry from the direct heat of the oven and will inhibit the pastry from puffing up properly. For convenience, you can freeze the unfilled baked puffs for up to 1 week. After thawing, pop the pastries into a hot oven for 3 to 5 minutes to crisp them before you fill them.

# CREAM PUFFS  Makes about sixteen 4-inch cream puffs

**PÂTE À CHOUX:**

1 cup water

½ cup (1 stick) unsalted butter,
  cut into 8 pieces

½ teaspoon salt

1 tablespoon sugar

1¼ cups sifted unbleached
  all-purpose flour

4 to 5 large eggs

Crème Chantilly (page 129)

Confectioners' sugar for dusting

1. Place an oven rack on the bottom shelf of the oven. Preheat the oven to 400°F. Use a nonstick baking sheet, or lightly grease a noninsulated baking sheet with solid shortening or butter and dust with flour. Turn the pan over and tap to remove any excess flour.

2. Combine the water, butter, salt, and sugar in a medium nonaluminum saucepan. Heat over medium heat, stirring occasionally until the butter melts completely. Do not allow the water to boil before the butter melts—this would upset the balance of moisture in the finished pastry.

3. Increase heat to high and bring the mixture to a full, rolling boil. Remove the pan from heat and add the flour to the pan all at once, stirring briskly with a wooden spoon until the dough pulls away from the sides of the pan and gathers in a clump around the spoon. (This batter is called a *panade*.)

4. Return the pan to medium heat and stir the batter briskly for 30 to 60 seconds. This will dry any excess moisture and eliminate any raw flour taste from the dough. Also, a drier base will be able to absorb more eggs, and the final cream puff will be lighter and crisper.

RECIPE CONTINUES >>

5. Line your countertop with a large piece of aluminum foil and empty the dough out onto the foil. Pat the dough into an 8-inch circle and let cool for 5 minutes. (If the batter is too hot, the eggs will start cooking before the pastry is baked, and the puffs won't be as light, puffy, and crisp as they should be.) Return the dough to the saucepan.

6. Crack 4 of the eggs into a medium bowl and beat with a fork until blended. Add one fourth of the eggs to the batter, stirring slowly so that the dough, which will separate slightly and become slippery, doesn't slop out of the pan. As the egg is incorporated into the dough, stir more briskly, just until the egg is incorporated. When the batter smooths out, incorporate another fourth of the beaten eggs. Repeat until all of the beaten eggs are incorporated into the batter.

7. The final batter should be smooth, slightly sticky, and malleable, but firm enough to form soft peaks and to be piped or scooped onto a baking sheet. If the batter seems too firm, beat the fifth egg and add it, 1 tablespoon at a time, to the batter, beating briskly. You don't want to add too much egg at this point; if the batter is too runny, the puffs will not rise properly.

8. Spoon heaping tablespoons of the batter onto the prepared pan, spacing them at least 2 inches apart. Bake for 20 minutes, or until the puffs are golden brown and expanded to three times their original size. Reduce the oven temperature to 350°F and continue baking for about 15 minutes to make sure the pastry is crisp, hollow, and dry inside. Remove the baking sheet from the oven and place on a wire rack.

9. Using a serrated knife, gently saw the puffs in half horizontally. This will release any steam from the pastries, preventing them from becoming soggy as they cool. Let cool completely.

10. Cream puffs are best filled as close to serving as possible, but they can be filled and refrigerated up to 4 hours before serving. Spoon 1/2 cup Crème Chantilly into the bottom half of each puff, or use a piping bag fitted with a 1/2-inch (No. 6) star tip to fill the cream puffs with a more decorative flourish. Replace each top and dust the cream puffs generously with confectioners' sugar. Serve immediately.

11. To freeze unfilled puffs, wrap them well in plastic wrap and store in a self-sealing plastic freezer bag or covered container to prevent them from absorbing any freezer odors.

# PÂTE À CHOUX

Pâte à choux is one of the oldest, most versatile, and easiest to master of all French pastries, requiring equipment no more complex than a heavy saucepan, a wooden spoon, and a little muscle. Pâte à choux pastry uses ordinary ingredients such as water, butter, flour, and eggs to deliver spectacular results. I still love watching the small blobs of dough go into the oven only to emerge as airy, hollow globes of crisp, puffed pastry ready to be stuffed with sweet and savory fillings. The *choux* in *Pâte à Choux* means "cabbage" in French, and this pastry was named, no doubt, by a French pastry chef with a whimsical bent, because the small baked puffs resemble tiny heads of cabbage.

**Profiteroles, tiny pâte à choux puffs** filled with ice cream and slathered with warm chocolate sauce, are a Parisian bistro classic. Combining both milk and water in the pâte à choux keeps these little frozen treats tender, even when they are served straight from the freezer. Profiteroles are a great dessert for a dinner party, because they can be made well in advance, as can the chocolate sauce, leaving you, the dessert queen, with nothing to do but smile and collect compliments.

# 𝒫ROFITEROLES   Makes about 3 dozen 2-inch puffs

⅔ cup water

⅓ cup milk

½ teaspoon salt

1 tablespoon sugar

½ cup (1 stick) unsalted butter, cut into 8 pieces

1¼ cups sifted unbleached all-purpose flour

4 to 5 large eggs

1 quart vanilla or coffee ice cream

Chocolate Sauce (page 134)

1. Place an oven rack on the bottom shelf of the oven. Preheat the oven to 400°F. Use a nonstick baking sheet, or lightly grease a noninsulated baking sheet with solid shortening or butter and dust with flour. Turn the pan over and tap to remove any excess flour.

2. Combine the water, milk, salt, sugar and butter in a medium nonaluminum saucepan. Heat over medium heat, stirring occasionally until the butter melts completely. Do not allow the water to boil before the butter melts—this would upset the balance of moisture in the finished pastry.

3. Increase heat to high and bring the mixture to a full, rolling boil. Remove the pan from heat and add the flour to the pan all at once, stirring briskly with a wooden spoon until the dough pulls away from the sides of the pan and gathers in a clump around the spoon.

4. Return the pan to medium heat and stir the batter briskly for 30 to 60 seconds. This will dry any excess moisture and eliminate any raw flour taste from the dough. Also, a drier base will be able to absorb more eggs, and the final pastry will be lighter and crisper.

5. Line your countertop with a large piece of aluminum foil and empty the dough out onto the foil. Pat the dough into an 8-inch circle and let cool for 5 minutes. (If the batter is too hot, the eggs will start cooking before the pastry is baked, and the puffs won't be as light, puffy, and crisp as they should be.) Return the dough to the saucepan.

RECIPE CONTINUES >>

Profiteroles

6. Crack 4 of the eggs into a medium bowl and beat with a fork until blended. Add one fourth of the eggs to the batter, stirring slowly so that the dough, which will separate slightly and become slippery, doesn't slop out of the pan. As the egg is incorporated into the dough, stir more briskly, just until the egg is incorporated. When the batter smooths out, incorporate another fourth of the beaten eggs. Repeat until all of the beaten eggs are incorporated into the batter.

7. The final batter should be smooth, slightly sticky, and malleable, but firm enough to form soft peaks and to be piped or scooped onto a baking sheet. If the batter seems too firm, beat the fifth egg and add it, 1 tablespoon at a time, to the batter, beating briskly. You don't want to add too much egg at this point; if the batter is too runny, the puffs will not rise properly.

8. Fill a piping bag fitted with a $\frac{1}{2}$-inch (No. 6) plain pastry tip with the batter. Pipe 1 to 1$\frac{1}{2}$-inch mounds at least 1 inch apart on the prepared pan. If the mounds develop a point as you pull the pastry tip away, wet your finger and pat the point down.

9. Bake for 20 minutes, or until the puffs are golden brown and expanded to three times their original size. Reduce the oven temperature to 350°F and continue baking for about 5 to 10 minutes to make sure the pastry is crisp, hollow, and dry inside. Remove the baking sheet from the oven and place on a wire rack.

10. Using a serrated knife, gently saw the puffs in half horizontally. This will release any steam from the pastries, preventing them from becoming soggy as they cool. Let cool completely.

11. When the puffs are completely cool, use a miniature ice cream scoop to fill the bottom half of each puff with ice cream. Place the pastry caps on top of the ice cream. Place the profiteroles in an airtight container and freeze for up to 3 days. Alternatively, you can freeze the puffs unfilled for up to 1 week. After thawing, pop the puffs in a hot oven for 3 to 5 minutes to crisp them up before you fill them.

12. To serve the profiteroles, create a pyramid by placing 3 in a shallow bowl or dish and place a fourth profiterole on top. Drizzle them liberally with warm chocolate sauce. Serve immediately.

**When I was in college, I made my first trip to Paris.** I was on a very strict budget that left little room for fine dinners, even at the sparest bistro. But I always had enough money to buy a little something at the many charcuteries and pâtisseries that peppered the city. I loved the French chocolate éclairs. I was very familiar with éclairs back home, but the French éclairs were so elegant, so trim, so neat and streamlined, unlike the big blowsy American versions that garishly spilled their whipped cream filling for all to see. French pastry chefs don't split the pastry to fill it; they pierce the baked pastry in an inconspicuous spot and pipe the pastry cream inside. The filled pastry is then dipped in a rich chocolate or coffee icing. These éclairs are rich, delicious, but not too large—just big enough for two or three bites.

This recipe makes a lot of éclairs, and they are impressive for a large party. Don't be intimidated! There are three components—the pastry, the pastry cream, and the icing—and none of them are difficult to execute. Bake the pastries a day or two ahead of time and freeze them. The pastry cream can be prepared from 1 day to 3 hours ahead of time, and the chocolate icing takes about 2 minutes to stir together. A little organization, a little confidence, and very little experience will have you enjoying these elegant little pastries in no time at all.

# *C*HOCOLATE *É*CLAIRS  Makes about 2 dozen 4-inch pastries

1 cup water

½ cup (1 stick) unsalted butter, cut into 8 pieces

½ teaspoon salt

1 tablespoon sugar

1¼ cups sifted unbleached all-purpose flour

4 to 5 large eggs

Pastry Cream or Coffee Pastry Cream (page 128)

Chocolate Icing (page 135) or Coffee Fondant Icing (page 136)

1. Place an oven rack on the bottom shelf of the oven. Preheat the oven to 400°F. Use a nonstick baking sheet, or lightly grease a noninsulated baking sheet with solid shortening or butter and dust with flour. Turn the pan over and tap to remove any excess flour.

2. Combine the water, butter, salt, and sugar in a medium nonaluminum saucepan. Heat over medium heat, stirring occasionally until the butter melts completely. Do not allow the water to boil before the butter melts—this would upset the balance of moisture in the finished pastry.

3. Increase heat to high and bring the mixture to a full, rolling boil. Remove the pan from heat and add the flour to the pan all at once, stirring briskly with a wooden spoon until the dough pulls away from the sides of the pan and gathers in a clump around the spoon.

4. Return the pan to medium heat and stir the batter briskly for 30 to 60 seconds. This will dry any excess moisture and eliminate any raw flour taste from the dough. Also, a drier base will be able to absorb more eggs, and the final cream puff will be lighter and crisper.

5. Line your countertop with a large piece of aluminum foil and empty the dough out onto the foil. Pat the dough into an 8-inch circle and let cool for 5 minutes. (If the batter is too hot, the eggs will start cooking before the pastry is baked, and the puffs won't be as light, puffy, and crisp as they should be.) Return the dough to the saucepan.

6. Crack 4 of the eggs into a medium bowl and beat with a fork until blended. Add one fourth of the eggs to the batter stirring slowly so that the dough, which will separate slightly and become slippery, doesn't slop out of the pan. As the egg is incorporated into the dough, stir more briskly, just until the egg is incorporated. When the batter smooths out, incorporate another fourth of the beaten eggs. Repeat until all of the beaten eggs are incorporated into the batter.

7. The final batter should be smooth, slightly sticky, and malleable, but firm enough to form soft peaks and to be piped or scooped onto a baking sheet. If the batter seems too firm, beat the fifth egg and add it, 1 tablespoon at a time, to the batter, beating briskly. You don't want to add too much egg at this point; if the batter is too runny, the puffs will not rise properly.

8. Fill a piping bag fitted with a 1/2-plain (No. 6) pastry tip with the batter. Pipe 4-inch strips of batter at least 2 inches apart on the prepared pan. Dip a fork in water and pat the strips of dough, smoothing out the tops of the pastry. Bake for 20 minutes, or until the pastry is crisp and golden and has risen to three times its original size. Reduce the oven temperature to 350°F and continue baking for 5 to 10 minutes, to make sure the pastry is crisp and hollow inside. Remove the éclairs from the oven and place the pan on a wire rack to cool. Pierce the end of each éclair with the tip of a sharp knife or with the tip of a bamboo skewer to release any interior steam from the pastry. Let cool completely.

9. Use the tip of a small paring knife to enlarge the holes in either end of each pastry. Fit a piping bag with a bismarck tip (No. 230)—used to fill doughnuts with jelly or pastry cream—or a 1/4-inch plain (No. 2) tip, and fill with pastry cream. Insert the tip into the éclair and fill the pastry with cream. If you are having difficulty getting the cream to fill the entire pastry, insert the pastry tip into the other end of the pastry and fill from that end as well. Fill the remaining pastries.

10. Dip the tops of the filled éclairs in the chocolate or coffee icing and let cool on a wire rack. Serve immediately, or store for up to 3 hours in a tightly covered container in the refrigerator.

# DEEP-FRYING

It isn't difficult to fry foods that are crisp on the outside, moist within, and grease-free. You just need to follow a few basic steps and use the right equipment for the job.

**The pan:** A large, cast-iron skillet works well; it isn't flimsy, and the cast iron conducts heat evenly and holds the heat well. Woks and Dutch ovens are also safe choices and work well because of their high sides. You can use commercial fryers as well, but make sure your fryer reaches 365°F for optimum frying. Make sure that any pan you use is wide enough and deep enough to hold plenty of oil for frying. Foods actually fry faster, lighter, and crisper and absorb less oil if they are surrounded by a large amount of hot oil as they fry. For safety's sake, use a pan that is large enough to hold at least 8 to 12 cups. You will only be filling it with 3 or 4 cups of oil, but you should allow plenty of room for the oil to bubble and splatter without being dangerous.

**The oil:** It is important to choose an oil that can stand the heat. Peanut oil is a great choice, as it can be heated up to 425°F before it starts to smoke and burn. Canola oil can also be used. It can't be heated to the same high temperature as peanut oil, but it can usually handle the temperature needed to fry foods that cook quickly, such as these beignets.

**The temperature:** The perfect temperature for optimum frying is between 365°F and 375°F. Fried foods absorb too much grease if they are cooked in oil below 340°F, and they will brown too quickly before the interior is cooked through if the oil rises above 375°F. The least stressful way to monitor the temperature is to use a deep-frying thermometer. If you don't have one, try the bread cube test: Cut a small cube of white bread and drop it in the hot oil. The bread will fry up golden brown in 1 minute at 350°F; at 375°F it will take 40 seconds.

**Note:** After frying, let the oil cool completely before discarding. It is best to discard the oil, as it can grow rancid quickly after its initial use.

**Beignets are nothing more exotic than pâte à choux deep-fried** to create lovely dumpling-like doughnuts that are crisp on the outside with a moist, custardy interior. Delicious! Roll them in cinnamon sugar or dust with confectioners' sugar, and you can close your eyes and pretend you're sitting in the Café du Monde in New Orleans. These beignets are great served with a dab of whipped cream for dessert, or with fresh fruit and café au lait for breakfast. Make sure you serve these while they are at their best—piping hot!

## ℬEIGNETS   Makes about 3 dozen beignets

¼ cup water

¾ cup milk

½ teaspoon salt

1 tablespoon sugar

½ cup (1 stick) unsalted butter, cut into 8 pieces

1¼ cups sifted unbleached all-purpose flour

4 to 5 large eggs

Peanut or canola oil for deep-frying

Cinnamon Sugar (recipe follows) for coating or confectioners' sugar for dusting

1. Combine the water, milk, salt, sugar, and butter in a medium nonaluminum saucepan. Heat over medium heat, stirring occasionally, until the butter melts completely. Do not allow the water to boil before the butter melts—this would upset the balance of moisture in the finished pastry.

2. Increase heat to high and bring the mixture to a full, rolling boil. Remove the pan from heat and add the flour to the pan all at once, stirring briskly with a wooden spoon until the dough pulls away from the sides of the pan and gathers in a clump around the spoon.

3. Return the pan to medium heat and stir the batter briskly for 30 to 60 seconds. This will dry any excess moisture and eliminate any raw flour taste from the dough.

4. Line your countertop with a large piece of aluminum foil and empty the dough out onto the foil. Pat the dough into an 8-inch circle and let cool for 5 minutes. Return the dough to the saucepan.

5. Crack 4 of the eggs into a medium bowl and beat with a fork until blended. Add one fourth of the eggs to the batter, stirring slowly so that the dough, which will separate slightly and become slippery, doesn't slop out of the pan. As the egg is incorporated into the dough, stir more briskly, just until the egg is incorporated. When the batter smooths out, incorporate another fourth of the beaten eggs. Repeat until all of the beaten eggs are incorporated into the batter.

RECIPE CONTINUES >>

Beignets

6. The final batter should be smooth, slightly sticky, and malleable, but firm enough to form soft peaks and to be piped or scooped onto a baking sheet. If the batter seems too firm, beat the fifth egg and add it, 1 tablespoon at a time, to the batter, beating briskly.

7. Preheat the oven to 200°F. Line a baking sheet with paper towels. Pour 3 inches of oil into a wok, large cast-iron skillet, Dutch oven, or deep fryer. Heat the oil over medium-high heat to 365°F.

8. Scoop 1 heaping tablespoon of the batter and carefully ease it into the hot fat. Cook 3 to 4 beignets at a time. Fry them, turning frequently, for 3 to 4 minutes, or until they are puffy and a deep golden brown. Using a wire-mesh skimmer, transfer the beignets to the paper towel–lined pan. While they are still hot, roll the beignets in the cinnamon sugar or dust liberally with confectioners' sugar. Serve immediately or place them on the baking sheet in the oven until ready to serve.

9. Check the temperature of the oil before repeating with the remaining batter. Serve warm beignets alone, or with Crème Chantilly or vanilla ice cream if you like.

# CINNAMON SUGAR

Stir 1 cup sugar and 3 tablespoons ground cinnamon together until completely combined.

**Substituting phyllo dough for the more traditional puff pastry in these Napoleons** (or *mille-feuilles* as they are known in France, which means "a thousand leaves") gives a modern spin to this classic dessert.

# *Nouveaux Napoleons*  Makes 6 napoleons

6 sheets phyllo dough, thawed
   if frozen

5 tablespoons unsalted butter,
   melted

5 tablespoons granulated sugar

Confectioners' sugar for dusting

Pastry Cream (page 128)

2 cups fresh raspberries or
   blueberries (optional)

Raspberry Coulis (page 135)

1. Place an oven rack on the middle shelf of the oven. Preheat the oven to 375°F. Line a baking sheet with parchment paper.

2. Lay 1 sheet of phyllo dough flat on a clean work surface. Lightly brush the phyllo with the melted butter, working from the edges towards the center. Sprinkle with 1 tablespoon of the granulated sugar. Layer the remaining 5 sheets of phyllo dough over the first, buttering and sprinkling all but the last sheet with 1 tablespoon granulated sugar. Dust the top sheet liberally with confectioners' sugar.

3. With a sharp knife or pizza wheel, cut the phyllo into 4 strips, each 3-by-17-inches. Cut each strip into thirds to make twelve 3-by-5½-inch rectangles.

4. Using a large metal spatula, transfer the phyllo rectangles to the prepared pan. Bake for 6 to 10 minutes, or until the phyllo is crisp and the confectioners' sugar has melted into a shiny, golden glaze. Remove the pan from the oven. Transfer the phyllo rectangles from the pan to a wire rack to cool. Serve immediately, or store in an airtight container for 1 to 2 days.

5. To assemble napoleons, place 1 phyllo rectangle on a dessert plate and spread with ½ cup pastry cream. If desired, sprinkle a few fresh raspberries or blueberries over the cream. Place a second phyllo rectangle on top of the cream, glazed side up. Repeat with the remaining 5 portions. Drizzle raspberry coulis around each napoleon and serve immediately.

Nouveaux Napoleons

# TARTS AND CAKES

## 2

WALKING DOWN A PARISIAN BOULEVARD, it is impossible to pass by the city's many pâtisseries without stopping to gaze at the impressive array of elegant tarts and cakes that grace their windows. Created daily to entice their patrons, sassy lemon tarts glow, lined up next to rich, caramelized Tartes Tatin. Moist quatre-quarts cakes, wrapped in shimmering cellophane, and glossy chocolate ganache tarts wait patiently to be boxed and beribboned, carried home, and enjoyed with a cup of freshly brewed tea. Bistros and cafés create their favorite versions of simple, moist cakes, and rustic tarts filled with warm chocolate custard, fragrant almond frangipane, or fresh fruits of the season. These pastry shop and bistro favorites can be duplicated easily in your own kitchen, bringing a little French panache into your repertoire of desserts.

The crust on this galette, a rustic, free-form fruit tart, is incredibly crisp and buttery. For a super flaky texture, freeze the butter, then grate it into the flour; small flakes of frozen butter yield a crisp, flaky pastry that still holds its shape when baked free-form style. Crème Chantilly or vanilla ice cream is a nice accompaniment to this tart.

# $\mathcal{A}$PPLE $\mathcal{G}$ALETTE  Makes one 10-inch tart; serves 6

### FLAKY PASTRY:

1 cup unbleached all-purpose flour

½ teaspoon salt

1 tablespoon sugar

½ cup (1 stick) unsalted butter, frozen solid

2 to 4 tablespoons ice water

### APPLE FILLING:

2 tablespoons flour

4 tablespoons granulated sugar

5 or 6 (about 1½ pounds) small Jonagold, Jonathan, Fuji, or Golden Delicious apples, peeled, cored, and cut into ¼-inch-thick slices (about 4 cups)

⅛ teaspoon freshly grated nutmeg

1 tablespoon Calvados, Cognac, or whiskey (optional)

1 tablespoon unsalted butter

### GLAZE:

1 egg white

2 tablespoons sugar

1. To make the pastry: In a medium bowl, stir together the flour, salt, and sugar.

2. Using the largest holes of a box grater, grate the frozen butter into long, thin shreds as quickly as possible, so it stays frozen. Toss the butter with the flour. If the butter seems to be softening, put the flour mixture in the freezer for a few minutes.

3. Use a fork or pastry blender to cut the grated butter into the flour a little more. Stir in 2 tablespoons water and combine quickly into a crumbly dough. If the dough seems too dry, add up to 2 more tablespoons of ice water, 1 tablespoon at a time. If you add more than 4 tablespoons water, the pastry may not be as flaky. On a lightly floured board, knead the pastry once or twice and pat into a flat disk. Wrap the pastry in plastic wrap and chill for at least 30 minutes. Line a baking sheet with parchment paper. Roll the dough between 2 large pieces of plastic wrap or waxed paper into a 12-inch round. Transfer the pastry to the prepared pan and remove the plastic or waxed paper. If the pastry seems to be getting too soft, return the rolled out dough to the refrigerator for a few minutes.

4. Place an oven rack on the bottom shelf of the oven. Preheat the oven to 400°F.

5. To make the filling: In a small bowl, stir together the flour and 1 tablespoon of the sugar. Spread over the pastry, leaving a 2-inch border uncovered.

6. Toss the sliced apples with the remaining 3 tablespoons sugar, the nutmeg, and the Calvados, Cognac, or whiskey, if using. Mound the fruit on the pastry. Cut the 1 tablespoon butter into small bits and dot the apples with it.

7. Fold the 2-inch border of the pastry over the apples, pleating as you go.

8. To glaze the galette: Brush the pastry with a little of the egg white. Sprinkle the entire galette—fruit and pastry both—with the sugar.

9. Bake the tart for 40 to 45 minutes, or until the apples are tender and the pastry is crisp and golden brown. Check the tart after 30 minutes; if the pastry and/or apples seem to be browning too quickly, cover loosely with aluminum foil and continue baking.

10. Remove the pan from the oven and place on a wire rack. Serve the galette warm or at room temperature.

# PERFECT FLAKY GALETTE PASTRY

1. **Freeze the butter:** Although the flavor of butter is exceptional, shortening has a higher melting point than butter and usually creates flakier pastry. For the best of both worlds—to duplicate the advantages of shortening but still maintain the superior flavor of butter— freeze it! According to food scientist Shirley Corriher, cold fats melt slower in the oven, allowing the pastry to set around it. As the fat starts to melt, the resulting steam lifts the layers of dough apart, creating flakes.

2. **Grate the butter:** With a free-form tart baked without a pie pan, like this galette, you want pastry that is flaky, but not so flaky that the pastry loses its shape while it is baking or shatters when the tart is sliced. To prevent this, grate frozen butter and cut it into the flour with a pastry blender. Smaller shreds of cold butter will deliver shorter flakes. The resulting pastry will be crisp, flaky, and delicious, but will hold its shape when baked, and afterward slice like a dream.

3. **Don't overwork the dough:** Your goal is to combine the ingredients as quickly as possible, working the dough as little as you can. Overworking the pastry will soften the butter and develop the gluten in the flour, resulting in a crust that is hard and tough instead of crisp and flaky. Be sure to use ice water too; this will also ensure that the butter stays cold and your crust stays flaky.

4. **Let it rest:** Let the dough rest for at least 30 minutes before rolling it out. Resting the dough ensures that the flour has completely absorbed the water, making it easier to roll out. This also allows less opportunity for overworking the dough. Rest the dough in the refrigerator for at least 30 minutes or up to 24 hours (well wrapped). If the dough is too firm, let it sit at room temperature until it is pliable enough to roll out easily.

There are many stories surrounding the unusual creation of the upside-down *Tarte des demoiselles Tatin*. In the early 1900s, two sisters from the town of Lamotte-Beuvron in France, forced to earn their own living due to reduced circumstances, started peddling their father's favorite pastry, an upside-down caramelized apple tart. Whether the sisters actually invented their famous tart or merely compounded its notoriety is open to debate. No matter how or why it was created, its delicious simplicity makes it a favorite. Tarte Tatin is delicious served alone or with vanilla ice cream.

# TARTE TATIN  Makes one 8- or 9-inch tart; serves 6 to 8

1¾ to 2 pounds (about 6 to 8) small crisp cooking apples (see list page 65), peeled, cored, and quartered

1 tablespoon fresh lemon juice

**CARAMEL:**

¾ cup sugar

1 tablespoon water

3 tablespoons unsalted butter

1 sheet (8 ounces) thawed frozen puff pastry, or Sweet Pastry Dough (page 137)

1. Place an oven rack on the bottom shelf of the oven. Preheat the oven to 425°F.

2. Toss the quartered apples with the lemon juice and set aside.

3. To make the caramel: Combine the sugar, water, and butter in a medium saucepan and cook, stirring occasionally, until the butter melts and the sugar dissolves and starts to turn color. Increase heat to high and let the mixture bubble until it turns a rich caramel brown, swirling the pan occasionally to make sure the sugar browns evenly. This should take about 4 to 5 minutes. Watch carefully; if the mixture gets too brown (about the color of a dirty penny), it will start to smoke and the resulting caramel will taste burned.

4. Pour the caramel into an 8- or 9-inch straight-sided cake pan. Drain any excess lemon juice from the apples. Place the apple quarters on their sides in the caramel, packing them very tightly in a ring around the edge of the cake pan. Place a second ring of apple quarters inside the first ring. In the very center, place 1 or 2 apple quarters, rounded sides down, in the caramel. Don't be afraid to pack the apples extremely close, shoving as many as you can into the pan. They will soften but hold their shape as they cook. This way there will be no empty spaces in the tart when it is inverted.

RECIPE CONTINUES >>

Tarte Tatin

5. Roll the puff pastry or flaky pastry out on a lightly floured board to the thickness of ¼ inch. Cut into a circle 1 inch larger than the cake pan. Lay the pastry over the apples, gently tucking the excess into the pan around the fruit. When baked, this will form a rim for the tart.

6. Bake for 30 to 35 minutes, or until the pastry is crisp and golden brown and the apples are tender. Insert a long bamboo skewer through a small gap in the pastry to test the apples—there should be no resistence to the skewer. Remove the tart from the oven and let rest for 5 to 7 minutes for the apples to reabsorb the juices.

7. Place a large serving plate over the tart. Invert the tart onto the plate and carefully remove the cake pan. If any apples stick to the pan, carefully remove them and replace them on the tart. Drizzle any excess caramel from the pan onto the tart. Serve immediately.

## CHOOSING THE RIGHT APPLE FOR BAKING

There are many delicious varieties of apples, but not all of them are right for cooking and baking. With the advent of wonderful farmer's markets, more and more varieties of apples are available. French apple tarts are usually made with a single crust and use very little, if any, thickener such as flour or cornstarch in their fillings. A good apple with the right texture and flavor is vital. When shopping, choose apples without blemishes or bruises. They should feel firm and heavy for their size. Since apples are usually harvested between September and November, apple desserts are perfect choices for cool autumn weather.

The following apple varieties are excellent for French pies and tarts. They are known for their firm, crisp flesh and aromatic balance of sweetness and acidity. When baking or cooking, these apples can stand the heat and will retain their shape while becoming meltingly tender in your favorite tart. You should be able to find at least a few of them in your local supermarket or farmer's market. Don't rely on one variety alone; experiment with different apples to see which ones have the best texture and flavor for you.

Jonathan

Northern Spy

Ida Red

Winesap

Golden Delicious

Jonagold

Gala

Rome Beauty

Mutsu/Crispin

**Frangipane, a delicious almond cream,** is said to have been created by French pastry chefs in honor of the sixteenth-century Italian nobleman Marquis Muzio Frangipani, who invented a technique to infuse gloves with the perfume of bitter almonds. His procedure was all the rage, and inspired pastry chefs to create a delicacy in his name. The flavor of almonds and fresh cherries have a magical affinity, and this simple-to-prepare almond tart takes advantage of the short season fresh cherries are available. Other fruits such as fresh plums, apricots, and poached pears or apples can also be used instead of the cherries with equal success.

# CHERRY-FRANGIPANE TART Makes one 9½-inch tart; serves 6 to 8

**FRANGIPANE CREAM:**

2 tablespoons flour

1 cup (4 ounces) slivered blanched almonds

½ cup granulated sugar

½ cup (1 stick) unsalted butter, softened

2 large eggs

½ teaspoon pure vanilla extract

¼ teaspoon pure almond extract

One 9 ½-inch partially baked Sweet Pastry Dough shell (page 137)

12 ounces fresh sweet cherries, such as Bing, pitted but left whole

Confectioners' sugar for dusting

Crème Chantilly (page 129), optional

1. Place a noninsulated baking sheet (an insulated baking sheet will prevent the pastry from browning properly) on a rack set on the bottom shelf of the oven. Preheat the oven to 375°F.

2. To make the frangipane cream: Combine the flour, almonds, and granulated sugar in a food processor. Grind until fine and powdery. Add the butter and process, using short pulses, just until blended and creamy. Add the eggs, vanilla, and almond extract and process until smooth.

3. Spoon the frangipane cream into the tart shell and spread smoothly. Arrange the cherries on top of the unbaked frangipane.

4. Place the tart pan on the baking sheet in the oven and bake for 40 to 45 minutes, or until the pastry is golden brown and the frangipane has risen around the fruit and is also golden brown. Insert a bamboo skewer into the frangipane to test for doneness; if it comes out clean, remove the tart from the oven.

5. Transfer the tart to a wire rack and let cool to room temperature. Dust with confectioners' sugar. Remove the tart from the outer rim, leaving it on the removable bottom. Transfer the tart to a serving platter, or slice and place individual servings on dessert plates. Serve alone or with Crème Chantilly.

Cherry-Frangipane Tart

Although using a wonderful European chocolate such as Valrhona or Callebaut, or the American Scharffen Berger chocolate, will raise this tart to new heights, don't let the price or unavailability of high-end chocolate stop you from baking this very simple and supremely elegant dessert. I have prepared the tart using either Nestlé or Guittard semisweet chocolate morsels and heard nothing but sighs of pleasure from those who sampled it.

# CHOCOLATE TRUFFLE TART  Makes one 9½-inch tart; serves 8

6 ounces semisweet or bittersweet chocolate, coarsely chopped, or semisweet chocolate morsels

1 cup heavy cream

2 tablespoons granulated sugar

1 tablespoon unsweetened Dutch-processed cocoa powder, plus more for dusting

½ teaspoon pure vanilla extract

2 tablespoons dark rum, Cognac, or whiskey (optional)

1 large egg

One 9½-inch partially baked Sweet Pastry Dough shell, (page 137)

Crème Chantilly (page 129)

1. Place a noninsulated baking sheet (do not use an insulated baking sheet—it will prevent the pastry from baking correctly) on the bottom shelf of the oven. Preheat the oven to 375°F.

2. Place the chocolate in a medium bowl. Combine cream and sugar in a medium saucepan. Sift the cocoa powder into the cream. Stir over medium heat until bubbles form around the edge of the pan and the cream is just about to come to a boil. Remove from heat and pour the cream over the chocolate. Let sit for about 30 seconds to soften the chocolate. Stir until smooth.

3. Whisk the vanilla; rum, Cognac, or whiskey (if using); and egg into the chocolate mixture until smooth. Pour the filling into the tart shell and place on the baking sheet in the oven. Bake for 12 to 15 minutes, or until just set. (The filling will firm up as it cools.)

4. Remove the baking sheet and tart from the oven. Place it on a wire rack and let the tart cool to room temperature. Dust with Dutch-processed cocoa powder. Remove the outer rim of the tart pan, leaving the tart on the removable bottom. Transfer to a serving platter, or slice and place individual servings on dessert plates. Serve with Crème Chantilly.

**One of my mother's favorite candies is See's chocolate-orange creams.** I created this dessert for her. A buttery chocolate pastry shell encloses a deep, rich chocolate ganache, and a sumptuous mousse, bursting with sweet orange flavor, is piped or spooned over the ganache before serving. This is a great recipe for entertaining, as both the ganache tart and the orange mousse can be made a day in advance.

# CAROLE'S TART Makes one 9 ½-inch tart; serves 8

One 9½-inch fully baked
  Sweet Chocolate Pastry
  shell (page 139)

Warm Chocolate Ganache
  (page 131) made with
  2 tablespoons Grand Marnier
  or other orange liqueur

**ORANGE MOUSSE:**

¼ cup frozen orange juice
  concentrate, thawed

Grated zest of 1 orange

¼ cup sugar

2 large eggs

4 tablespoons unsalted butter,
  softened

½ cup heavy cream, whipped
  to soft peaks

Unsweetened Dutch-processed
  cocoa powder or chocolate
  curls for garnish

1. Pour the warm ganache through a fine-meshed sieve into the chocolate tart shell. Shake gently to allow the filling to settle into the pastry shell in an even layer. Refrigerate the tart until the filling is firm, 1 to 2 hours. Remove the tart from the refrigerator and let it come to room temperature before serving.

2. To make the orange mousse: Fill a large sauté pan or skillet half full with warm water. Place over medium-high heat and bring to a simmer.

3. Combine all the ingredients except the whipped cream in a medium stainless steel bowl. Place the bowl in the simmering water and stir constantly with a whisk or wooden spoon for 7 to 10 minutes, or until the butter melts and the mixture is thick and smooth, with a soft puddinglike texture.

4. Remove the bowl from the hot water and pour the orange cream through a fine-meshed sieve into a clean bowl. Cover with plastic wrap, pressing it onto the surface of the cream to prevent a skin from forming. Pierce the plastic wrap with a few holes to allow steam to escape. Refrigerate until completely cold. Fold the softly whipped cream into the orange cream until smooth. Do not overmix. The orange mousse can be prepared up to this point, covered, and chilled for up to 24 hours.

5. Fit a piping bag with a ½-inch (No. 6) star pastry tip and fill it with the orange mousse. Pipe the orange mousse over the surface of the ganache in a decorative design. Alternatively, slice the tart and place on dessert plates. Spoon a large dollop of orange mousse on each slice and dust with cocoa powder or sprinkle with chocolate curls. Serve immediately.

The first time my husband and I went to Paris together, we arrived very late at night, when most of the area where we were staying was shuttered tight. Our hotel, La Louisiane, on the rue de Seine, is right in the heart of the city. The next morning we peeked out our window to see a street market alive with merchants hawking cheeses, baskets of strawberries, fat white asparagus, and fresh tulips in a rainbow of colors. I snapped a picture of a large man wearing a dusty blue smock and jaunty beret surrounded by mounds of wild mushrooms. A small bohemian cafe called La Palette is tucked into a picturesque corner near this lively street market. The walls are decorated with artists' palettes and the work of local painters. One of their house specialties is a sunny lemon tart, like this one.

# Lemon Tart  Makes one 9½-inch tart; serves 8

¾ cup fresh lemon juice

Grated zest of 3 or 4 lemons

1¼ cups sugar

5 large eggs

4 egg yolks

12 tablespoons unsalted butter, softened

One 9½-inch fully baked Sweet Pastry Dough shell (page 137)

1. Place an oven rack on the middle shelf of the oven. Preheat the oven to 375°F.

2. Fill a large sauté pan or skillet half full with warm water. Place over medium-high heat and bring to a simmer.

3. In a medium stainless steel bowl, combine the lemon juice, zest, sugar, eggs, and yolks and whisk until smooth. Add the softened butter. The mixture will now have a curdled appearance; don't worry, it will smooth out as it cooks and the butter melts.

4. Place the bowl in the simmering water and stir constantly with a whisk or wooden spoon for 7 to 10 minutes, or until the butter melts and the mixture is thick and smooth, with a soft, pudding-like texture.

5. Remove the bowl from the hot water and pour the lemon cream through a fine-meshed sieve into the pastry shell. Use a small palette knife or offset spatula to spread it evenly.

6. Place the tart on a baking sheet and bake for 10 to 12 minutes, or until the filling is set but not browned. Remove the baking sheet from the oven and cool completely on a wire rack.

Lemon Tart

I **developed this sumptuous orange tart** after I tasted a tart à l'orange in Gerard Mulot's St-Germaine pâtisserie in Paris. The tart has a crackly sugar topping reminiscent of crème brûlée. Orange cream is softer than its tarter cousin, lemon cream, so you may want to prepare individual tartlets instead of a single, larger tart.

# BURNISHED ORANGE TART
Makes one 9½-inch tart or four 4¾-inch tartlets

6 tablespoons frozen orange juice concentrate, thawed

2 tablespoons fresh lemon juice

Grated zest of 3 oranges

½ cup sugar, plus 6 tablespoons sugar for topping

5 large eggs

8 tablespoons unsalted butter, softened

1 tablespoon Grand Marnier or other orange liqueur

One 9½-inch fully baked Sweet Pastry Dough tart shell, or four 4¾-inch fully baked Sweet Pastry Dough tartlet shells (page 137)

1. Fill a large sauté pan or skillet half full with warm water. Place over medium-high heat and bring to a simmer.

2. Combine the orange juice concentrate, lemon juice, orange zest, ½ cup sugar, and eggs in a medium stainless steel bowl and whisk together until smooth. Whisk the softened butter into the egg mixture. The mixture will now have a curdled appearance; don't worry, it will smooth out as it cooks and the butter melts.

3. Place the bowl with the orange mixture in the pan of simmering water and stir constantly with a whisk or wooden spoon for 7 to 10 minutes, or until the butter melts and the mixture is thick and smooth, with a soft puddinglike texture. Whisk in the liqueur.

4. Remove the bowl from the hot water and pour the orange cream through a fine-meshed sieve into a cool bowl. Cover the cream with plastic wrap, pressing the plastic onto the surface of the cream to prevent a skin from forming, and piercing it with a few holes to allow steam to escape. Refrigerate the cream for at least 3 hours or up to 24 hours.

5. Assemble the tart or tartlets up to 1 hour before you are ready to serve: Fill the shell(s) with orange cream and spread it smooth, using a small icing spatula or offset spatula. Sprinkle the top of the tart or tartlets with sugar (6 tablespoons for the larger tart and 1 tablespoon each for the tartlets) and heat with a small propane or butane torch until the sugar melts, forming a smooth, thin layer of crisp, caramelized sugar. Or, place the tart(s) on a baking sheet and heat under a preheated broiler for 1 to 2 minutes.

Burnished Orange Tart

**Ripe black cherries from Ixtassou in rugged French Basque country** are picked by the bushel every summer and immediately preserved for use throughout the year. Sour cherry preserves are served often with cheese and bread, or as a filling in this moist, rich cake. Use sour cherry preserves made in France, if you can find them.

# Basque Cake

Makes one 10-inch cake; serves 8 to 10

1 cup (2 sticks) unsalted butter, softened

1⅓ cups granulated sugar

3 large eggs

1 teaspoon pure vanilla extract

2¾ cups cake flour

¼ teaspoon salt

1 teaspoon baking powder

⅓ cup sour cherry preserves

⅛ teaspoon pure almond extract (optional)

¼ cup sliced almonds (optional)

Confectioners' sugar for dusting

1. Place an oven rack on the middle shelf of the oven. Preheat the oven to 325°F. Spray a 10-inch cake pan or spring-form pan with nonstick vegetable-oil cooking spray.

2. Using an electric mixer, beat the butter until creamy. Gradually beat in the sugar until light and fluffy. Add the eggs, one at a time, beating well after each addition. Beat in the vanilla extract.

3. Sift the cake flour, salt, and baking powder together and use a rubber spatula to fold the dry ingredients into the butter mixture until a soft dough forms and no white streaks of flour remain.

4. Spread half the batter evenly in the bottom of the prepared pan. Stir the almond extract, if using, into the cherry preserves. Spoon the cherry preserves over the batter, spreading it within 2 inches of the border.

5. Drop the remaining batter by large spoonfuls over the preserves. Spread the batter carefully over the jam to the edge of the pan. Sprinkle with sliced almonds, if using.

6. Bake for 40 to 50 minutes, or until a bamboo skewer inserted into the cake comes out with a few moist crumbs clinging to it. Let cool in the pan on a wire rack. Unmold the cake and dust with confectioners' sugar.

Basque Cake

**Quatre-Quarts, or "four quarters," cake,** was so named because it was originally made with equal weights flour, sugar, eggs, and butter. This version is a light, moist pound cake with a mild almond flavor scented with dark rum. It tastes even better the day after it is baked, and is a perfect light dessert or tea cake.

# QUATRE-QUARTS CAKE
Makes one 8½-by-4½-inch loaf cake; serves 8

½ cup (1 stick) unsalted butter, softened

½ cup sugar

2 large eggs

2 teaspoons pure vanilla extract

2 tablespoons dark rum

¾ cup cake flour

½ cup sliced almonds

½ teaspoon baking powder

¼ teaspoon salt

1. Place an oven rack on the middle shelf of the oven. Preheat the oven to 325°F. Spray an 8½-by-4½-inch loaf pan with nonstick vegetable-oil cooking spray.

2. Using an electric mixer, beat the butter until creamy. Gradually beat in the sugar until light and fluffy. Add the eggs, one at a time, beating well after each addition. Beat in the vanilla and dark rum.

3. Combine the cake flour and the almonds in a food processor and grind until fine and powdery. Add the baking powder and salt and pulse once to combine.

4. Using a large rubber spatula, fold the dry ingredients into the butter mixture until no streaks of flour remain.

5. Spread the batter evenly in the prepared pan and bake for 30 to 35 minutes, or until a skewer inserted in the center of the cake comes out with a few moist crumbs sticking to it.

6. Let cool on a wire rack for 5 minutes. Unmold and let cool completely.

# CREAMING BUTTER AND SUGAR

Light, tender, fine-grained butter cakes depend on creaming, or mixing butter and sugar together completely, for their superior texture. Creaming butter and sugar together does more than create a batter that is smooth and lump free. Creaming incorporates air bubbles into the batter. These air bubbles form the first stepping stone in leavening cakes. The addition of eggs or chemical leavening agents (like baking powder or baking soda) enlarge the bubbles incorporated into the batter through creaming, causing the cake to rise in the oven when baked. Adequate creaming ensures baked goods with a silky texture and a delicate crumb.

**STEPS FOR PERFECT CREAMING:**

1. Always use soft butter at room temperature; it mixes more easily with the sugar, making it easier to incorporate air into the mixture.

2. Beat the butter alone to lighten it a little, then add the sugar gradually. As the sugar crystals cut into the butter, small air pockets form, increasing the volume of the mixture.

3. Beat the butter and sugar for about 5 minutes; the mixture should become a pale, creamy yellow and increase in volume. When the sugar crystals are barely visible, you'll know you've got it right.

**This cake is airy and moist, with an intense chocolate flavor.** It combines all the wonderful qualities of a chocolate soufflé without the anxiety. This cake needs to settle slightly before serving, and it is delicious both warm and at room temperature. You can even chill it for a creamy, slightly fudgy texture. Serve slices of this cake with crème Anglaise, or vanilla, fresh mint, or coffee ice cream. Add caramel or warm chocolate sauce and let the bacchanal begin!

# ℱALLEN ℂHOCOLATE-ℐOUFFLÉ ℂAKE

Makes one 10-inch cake; serves 10 to 12

1 pound semisweet or bittersweet chocolate, coarsely chopped, or semisweet chocolate morsels

1 cup (2 sticks) unsalted butter, cut into 16 pieces, plus 2 tablespoons melted butter for coating cake pan

8 large eggs, separated, at room temperature

Pinch of salt

¾ cup superfine sugar, plus more for coating cake pan

2 tablespoons Cognac, dark rum, or whiskey

1 teaspoon pure vanilla extract

½ teaspoon cream of tartar

Crème Anglaise (page 126) or French Vanilla Ice Cream (page 115) for serving

Caramel Sauce (page 133) or Chocolate Sauce (page 134), (optional)

1. Place an oven rack on the middle shelf of the oven. Preheat the oven to 350°F. Brush a 10-inch spring-form pan with melted butter and coat the bottom and sides of the pan with superfine sugar. Tap out any excess sugar.

2. In a double boiler over barely simmering water, melt together the chocolate and 1 cup butter. Stir until smooth. Or, combine the chocolate and butter in a microwave-safe bowl. Heat, uncovered, on medium power for 1½ to 4 minutes, until the butter melts and the chocolate becomes soft and shiny. Remove the bowl from the microwave and stir until chocolate is completely melted and thoroughly combined with the butter. Set aside.

**RECIPE CONTINUES >>**

Fallen Chocolate-Soufflé Cake

3. In a large bowl, using a hand-held mixer set at medium speed, beat the egg yolks and salt until blended. Gradually add $\frac{1}{4}$ cup sugar and beat for 4 to 6 minutes, or until the mixture is pale yellow and forms a slowly dissolving ribbon on the surface of the batter when the beaters are lifted. Whisk in the Cognac and vanilla. Gradually whisk the egg yolk mixture into the melted chocolate.

4. In a large, clean bowl, beat the egg whites and cream of tartar with an electric mixer at low speed until foamy. Increase the mixer speed to medium-high and continue beating until the whites become opaque and form soft mounds in the bowl. Continue beating, adding the remaining $\frac{1}{2}$ cup sugar 1 tablespoon at a time, until soft peaks form.

5. Stir one third of the beaten egg whites into the chocolate batter to soften it. Using a rubber spatula, gently fold in the remaining egg whites just until blended.

6. Spoon the chocolate batter into the prepared pan. Bake for 25 to 35 minutes, or until the cake appears puffy and firm. The cake should still be moist but not liquid in the center, so a bamboo skewer inserted into the cake *should not* come out clean.

7. Remove the cake from the oven and cool on a wire rack for 15 minutes. It will fall slightly as it cools. Remove the sides of the pan. Slice and serve the cake slightly warm or at room temperature with Crème Anglaise or ice cream. Drizzle with caramel and chocolate sauces, if using.

## FEARLESS FOLDING

Folding delicate ingredients together correctly is vital for perfect soufflés, mousses, and other fragile desserts. These tips should help.

1. **Use the right tool:** Use a large rubber spatula to fold the ingredients together without deflating the beaten egg whites.

2. **Keep it light:** If you are folding beaten egg whites into a heavier base, make sure you add the whites to the base or batter and not the other way around–pouring a heavy batter onto the delicate beaten whites will deflate them, and the cake or soufflé will not rise as high.

3. **Up and over:** With a large rubber spatula, cut straight down into the center of the bowl, scooping the mixture up from the bottom of the bowl and lifting it over the top of the mixture. Give the bowl a half turn and continue to fold the mixture up and over itself to incorporate the ingredients. Continue the process until the ingredients are combined.

4. **Know when to stop:** It isn't vital that every single bit of egg white is folded into the base completely; it's better to err on the side of safety and stop folding even if a spot or two of egg whites remain, then to deflate the mixture by overworking it.

**I developed this simple but attractive tart** after spying a similar one displayed in the pâtisserie at Fauchon in Paris. I snapped a picture of the *tart macaronnade et fraises* before I was shooed away by a suspicious saleswoman.

# STRAWBERRY MACAROON TART   Makes one 8-inch tart; serves 8

1⅓ cups slivered blanched
  almonds

¾ cup sugar

2 large egg whites

½ teaspoon pure vanilla extract

**APRICOT GLAZE:**

½ cup apricot jam

1 tablespoon fresh lemon juice
  or water

2 to 4 cups fresh strawberries,
  hulled

2 tablespoons finely chopped
  pistachios

1. Place an oven rack on the middle shelf of the oven. Preheat the oven to 350°F. Line a baking sheet with parchment paper. Place an 8-inch cake pan on the parchment and trace around the bottom of the pan with a pen or pencil. Turn the paper over on the baking sheet so that you can see the outline but the almond paste will not come in contact with the markings when you pipe the mixture onto the parchment.

2. Combine the almonds and sugar in a food processor and grind until fine and powdery. Transfer to a medium bowl.

3. In a separate bowl, beat the egg whites and vanilla together with a wire whisk until frothy.

4. Stir enough of the egg white into the almond mixture to form a paste that is soft and smooth enough to pipe, but firm enough to hold its shape. To test, use a spoon to scoop out a dollop of the paste from the center of the bowl:

The paste should be easy to scoop, but the mixture remaining in the bowl should not ooze together to close the indentation made by the spoon.

5. Fit a piping bag with a ½-inch (No. 6) star pastry tip. Fill the piping bag with the almond paste. Pipe a spiral of almond paste onto the baking sheet, starting from the center of the penciled circle and moving towards the outer rim.

RECIPE CONTINUES >>

Strawberry Macaroon Tart

6. Bake for about 20 minutes, or until it is firm and just beginning to brown.

7. Meanwhile, make the apricot glaze: Combine the apricot jam and lemon juice in a small saucepan. Heat the jam over medium heat until it melts and starts to boil. Pour the jam through a fine-meshed sieve into a small bowl to remove any bits of apricot pulp.

8. Remove the almond tart from the oven and place the pan on a wire rack to cool. When cool enough to handle, use a large metal spatula to transfer the tart to a serving plate.

9. Brush the tart with the hot apricot glaze to give it a shiny finish.

10. Cut all but 1 of the strawberries in half lengthwise. Place the whole strawberry, pointed end up, in the center of the tart. Arrange the sliced strawberries, pointed ends up, around the whole strawberry as if they were petals in a flower. Brush the berries with the apricot glaze and sprinkle with the chopped pistachios.

11. The tart can sit at room temperature in a cool place for up to 1 hour before serving. If not serving immediately, refrigerate for up to 12 hours. Remove from the refrigerator about 30 minutes before serving. You can also make the almond base 1 day in advance and store in an airtight container. Right before serving, brush it with hot apricot glaze and arrange the strawberry "petals" on top.

**Can't decide between serving dessert or a cheese course after dinner?** This goat-cheese cake, with its mildly tart flavor and crunchy hazelnut coating, is a delicious way to satisfy both cravings.

# GOAT-CHEESE CAKE WITH GLAZED FIGS

Makes one 8-inch cake; serves 8 to 10

4 ounces fresh mild goat cheese
at room temperature

8 ounces cream cheese at
room temperature

¼ cup heavy cream

1 tablespoon fresh lemon juice

Grated zest of 1 lemon

1 teaspoon pure vanilla extract

4 large eggs

¾ cup sugar

2 tablespoons flour

½ cup hazelnuts, toasted,
skinned and finely chopped
(see page 19)

Glazed Figs (recipe follows)

1. Place an oven rack on the middle shelf of the oven. Preheat the oven to 325°F. Spray the cake pan with nonstick vegetable-oil cooking spray or brush lightly with vegetable oil. Line the cake pan with a circle of parchment paper.

2. Combine the goat cheese and cream cheese in a medium bowl and beat with an electric mixer set at medium speed until smooth. Beat in the cream, lemon juice, zest, and vanilla until creamy. Set aside.

3. In a large bowl, using a hand-held mixer set at medium speed, beat the eggs until blended. Gradually add the sugar and beat 4 to 6 minutes, or until the mixture is pale yellow and forms a slowly dissolving ribbon on its surface when the beaters are lifted. On low speed, gradually beat the flour and then the cheese mixture into the eggs until smooth and creamy.

4. Pour the batter into the prepared pan. Place the cake pan in a 9-by-13-inch baking pan and pour boiling water into the baking pan until it comes halfway up the outside of the cake pan.

5. Bake the cheesecake for 35 to 45 minutes, or until the cheesecake is firm and slightly golden on top.

6. Remove the cheesecake from the oven and the 9-by-13-inch baking pan, and let cool completely on a wire rack. Cover the cheesecake with plastic wrap and refrigerate until cold, at least 3 hours or up to 24 hours. Invert the cheesecake onto a serving platter and remove the parchment paper liner. Press the chopped hazelnuts generously on the top and around the sides of the cheesecake. To serve, slice into wedges. Serve each slice with a spoonful of glazed figs, drizzling the plate with a little of the poaching syrup.

**Glazed figs are delicious with goat-cheese cake,** but they are also wonderful served with a scoop of vanilla or caramel ice cream.

## *GLAZED FIGS*  Makes 2 cups

1 cup sugar

1 cup water

3 tablespoons dark rum

1 vanilla bean, halved lengthwise

1 cinnamon stick

1 strip lemon zest

8 ounces dried Calmyrna figs

1. Combine the sugar and water in a large saucepan. Bring to a boil. Reduce heat and simmer for 5 minutes, or until slightly thickened.

2. Add the rum, vanilla bean, cinnamon stick, and strip of lemon zest and simmer another 5 minutes.

3. Slice the figs in half and add to the sugar syrup. Simmer the figs, uncovered, for 20 to 30 minutes, or until they are soft but still retain their shape.

4. Remove the pan from heat and let the figs cool completely in the sugar syrup.

When my friend Mary Ann and I recently visited Paris, one of the first places I wanted to take her was Fauchon, an FAO Schwarz for food lovers. Stocked with more than twenty thousand items, from tropical fruits and exotic teas to foie gras and truffle oil, fruit preserves, and bottled mustard fruits, Fauchon is the most luxurious food pavilion in Paris. The enchanting centerpiece of this food mecca is the pâtisserie. Elaborate cakes and tarts, pyramids of candied fruits, and tiny pastries are displayed like crown jewels. When I tried to take a picture of this fabulous abundance, a woman behind the counter cried *"Non, non, madame!"* and waved my camera away. Even pastries are protected from paparazzi, I guess.

Fauchon's delicacies can be sampled in their tearoom. Perusing the pastry case, we saw a glass bowl with a mysterious lump smothered in raspberry coulis. What was it? Unable to stand the mystery, we bypassed more elaborate confections and ordered the *diplomat*. Two bites into the very moist, slightly sweet cake, the lightbulb went off: bread pudding! When preparing this pudding use very dry brioche cubes; the drier your bread is, the more milk it will absorb, yielding a delightfully moist, firm, fine-textured pudding. Serve cold, with raspberry coulis, lots of crème anglaise, or caramel sauce.

# DIPLOMAT PUDDING CAKE   Makes one 8-inch cake; serves 8

One 8-ounce brioche loaf, cubed (about 4 cups) and dried overnight until hard and crisp

⅓ cup raisins or finely diced dried apricots (optional)

¼ cup dark rum, Cognac, or Grand Marnier

1 large egg

5 egg yolks

½ cup firmly packed light brown sugar

½ cup granulated sugar, plus more for the cake pan

2¾ cups milk

1 teaspoon pure vanilla extract

Raspberry Coulis (page 135) or Crème Anglaise (page 126) or Caramel Sauce (page 133)

1. Place an oven rack on the middle shelf of the oven. Preheat the oven to 350°F. Grease an 8-inch cake pan with softened butter and sprinkle granulated sugar on the bottom and sides of the cake pan. Tap out any excess sugar.

2. In a small saucepan, combine the raisins or apricots and dark rum, Cognac, or Grand Marnier. Warm over low heat, but do not boil. Remove from heat and set aside to let the fruit absorb the spirits.

3. In a large bowl, whisk the egg, egg yolks, and sugars together until smooth and combined. Heat the milk in a medium saucepan until bubbles form around the edges and the milk is ready to boil. Whisk $1/2$ cup of the milk into the eggs. Slowly whisk the remaining milk into the eggs until smooth. Stir in the vanilla.

4. Add the bread cubes, raisins or apricots, and rum, Cognac, or Grand Marnier to the milk mixture. Stir to coat the cubes. Let sit for at least 1 hour for the bread to absorb the custard mixture.

5. Pour the mixture into the prepared pan and place it in a 9-by-13-inch baking pan. Pour boiling water into the baking pan until it reaches halfway up the sides of the cake pan. Bake for approximately 50 to 60 minutes, or until the cake is firm and a knife inserted into the center comes out clean.

6. Remove the cake pan from the baking pan and place it on a wire rack to cool. The pudding can be served at room temperature, but I think it is best served cold. Cover and refrigerate for at least 1 hour or up to 24 hours.

7. Serve slices of the diplomat smothered in Raspberry Coulis or Crème Anglaise, or drizzled with Caramel Sauce.

Originally created by the great pastry chef Gaston Lenôtre, this uncommon cake layers crisp chocolate meringue with a rich chocolate mousse. The meringue and the mousse can both be prepared ahead of time. Assemble the cake at least 1 hour or up to 1 day before you want to serve it.

# CONCORDE
Makes one 8-inch cake; serves 8 to 10

## CHOCOLATE MERINGUE:

6 egg whites, at room temperature

½ teaspoon cream of tartar

1 cup superfine sugar

½ teaspoon pure vanilla extract

1 cup confectioners' sugar, sifted

¼ cup unsweetened Dutch processed cocoa powder

Pinch of salt

## EASY CHOCOLATE MOUSSE:

9 ounces semisweet chocolate, coarsely chopped, or semisweet chocolate morsels

2 cups heavy cream

2 teaspoons instant coffee or espresso powder dissolved in 2 teaspoons hot water

Confectioners' sugar and unsweetened Dutch processed cocoa powder for dusting

1. Place an oven rack on the middle shelf of the oven and the second rack on the top shelf. Preheat the oven to 200°F. Line 2 baking sheets with parchment paper. On the first baking sheet, trace two 8-inch circles on the parchment paper, using the bottom of an 8-inch cake pan as a template. Trace a third circle on the second baking sheet. Turn the parchment paper over on the baking sheets so that you can see the outline but the meringue won't come in contact with the markings when you pipe it onto the parchment.

2. To make the meringue: In a large bowl, beat the egg whites and cream of tartar with an electric mixer at low speed until foamy. Increase the mixer speed to medium high and continue beating until soft peaks form. Continue beating, adding the superfine sugar 1 tablespoon at a time, until stiff, glossy peaks form. Beat in the vanilla.

3. Sift the confectioners' sugar, cocoa powder, and salt together. Using a rubber spatula, carefully fold the cocoa mixture into the meringue just until no streaks of cocoa remain. Do not fold the cocoa mixture in any more than is necessary, as overmixing will deflate the meringue. You want the mixture to hold stiff peaks, which ensures that the meringue disks will hold their shape.

4. Fit a 16- or 18-inch piping bag with a $3/8$-inch (No. 5) plain tip. Fill the bag with the meringue. Starting from the center of each circle, squeeze out the meringue in a spiral. Pipe the remaining meringue into long strips on the baking sheet with 1 meringue circle.

5. Bake the meringues for 2 hours, or until crisp. If the oven seems too hot, or the meringues are beginning to color, reduce the oven temperature to 175°F and prop the oven door open slightly with the handle of a wooden spoon. Turn the oven off and let the meringues cool in the oven for 1 hour. Cut the meringue strips into $1/4$- to $1/2$-inch pieces.

6. To make the chocolate mousse: Place the chopped chocolate in a medium bowl.

7. In a small saucepan, combine $3/4$ cup of the cream with the coffee mixture. Heat over medium heat until bubbles start to form around the edges of the pan and the cream is just about to boil. Immediately pour the hot cream over the chocolate and let sit for about 30 seconds to soften the chocolate. Stir until smooth.

8. Let the chocolate mixture cool until it is at room temperature but still malleable. In a large bowl, beat the remaining $1 1/4$ cups cream until soft peaks form. Using a rubber spatula, fold the whipped cream into the chocolate mixture until thoroughly blended.

9. To assemble: Place 1 meringue circle on a serving plate. With a small palette knife or offset spatula, spread one third of the mousse over the surface of the meringue. Cover with a second circle of meringue and spread with another one third of the mousse. Place the final meringue disk on top of the cake. Frost the top and the sides of the cake with the remaining mousse. Press the broken meringue sticks into the top and sides of the cake. Dust the entire cake with confectioners' sugar and cocoa powder. Refrigerate for at least 1 hour or up to 1 day before serving. The meringue will soften slightly the longer it sits in the refrigerator, but remains just as delicious.

# HOT, COLD, AND CREAMY

# 3

THE SIMPLE, UNDERSTATED DESSERTS OFFERED with most prix fixe menus in French bistros and brasseries are among the easiest French desserts to prepare at home. Warm fruit gratins, caramel-glazed custards, and luscious, chocolate- or coffee-infused pots de crème are among my favorite French comfort foods.

Inspired by Berthillon, the supreme purveyor of ice creams and sorbets in Paris, I've also developed recipes for deliciously different and easy homemade frozen treats. Berthillon supplies many restaurants in Paris with exotic ice cream flavors from mango and passion fruit to *nougat au miel* and coconut; perfect served alone or in *coupes*, ice cream is always a favorite. Try a *café Liégeois*, a popular Parisian ice cream treat featuring coffee ice cream smothered in warm chocolate sauce and freshly whipped cream, or assemble my version of the classic *poires belle Hélène*, luscious caramel-poached pears filled with vanilla ice cream and drizzled with caramel or chocolate sauce. Unforgettable.

**Crêpes are fast and simple to make.** The batter can—and should—be made in advance. It has to rest for at least 2 hours for the flour to absorb the liquid and soften, ensuring a delicate, tender crêpe. The crêpes themselves can be made 2 days in advance and reheated gently in a buttered pan before being filled with the caramelized apples. Cinnamon is not used very often in French desserts, and I prefer to let the flavor of the apples shine through alone, but if you love cinnamon, add ¼ teaspoon to the apples while they are cooking.

# $\mathcal{W}$ARM $\mathcal{A}$PPLE $\mathcal{C}$RÊPES   Makes 16 to 18 crepes; serves 8 to 9

**CRÊPE BATTER:**

3 large eggs

1 cup milk

¼ cup water

3 tablespoons butter, melted

1¼ cups unbleached
    all-purpose flour

¼ teaspoon salt

1 tablespoon sugar

Vegetable oil for cooking crêpes

**APPLE FILLING:**

8 crisp apples (about 2 pounds)
    such as Jonathan, Jonagold,
    Gala, Golden Delicious, or
    Mutsu/Crispin

⅓ cup granulated sugar

2 tablespoons fresh lemon juice

2 tablespoons unsalted butter

1 cup sour cream sweetened
    with 3 tablespoons light
    brown sugar, or 1 pint vanilla
    or caramel ice cream

Confectioners' sugar for dusting

RECIPE CONTINUES >>

Warm Apple Crêpes

1. To make the batter: To a blender, add the eggs, milk, water, melted butter, flour, salt, and sugar, in that order. Blend until smooth. Pour the batter through a fine-meshed sieve into a large bowl. Cover and refrigerate for at least 2 hours or overnight.

2. Let the batter come to room temperature. Heat an 8-inch nonstick crêpe pan or skillet over medium heat. Using a pastry brush, very lightly coat the pan with vegetable oil. Using a 1/4-cup measuring cup or a small ladle, pour 3 tablespoons batter into the pan. Lift the pan off heat and swirl the batter over the bottom and edges of the pan in a thin, even layer. Cook for 1 1/2 to 2 minutes, or until the edges of the crêpe start to pull away from the pan and lightly brown.

3. With your fingers, a fork, or a small offset spatula, carefully slip the crêpe out of the pan and turn it over. Cook the other side for 20 or 30 seconds and transfer the crêpe to a nearby serving platter. If the crêpes seem to be browning too much, reduce the heat slightly.

4. Repeat to cook the remaining batter, brushing the pan with oil after every 2 or 3 crêpes. Use the crêpes immediately, or let cool completely, wrap well, and store in the refrigerator for 1 or 2 days. To reheat the crêpes, brush a nonstick pan with a little melted butter and heat the crêpes, one at a time, until warmed through.

5. To make the filling: Peel, core, and cut the apples into 1/4-inch slices.

6. Stir the granulated sugar and lemon juice together in a large sauté pan or skillet and cook until the sugar melts and starts to turn a light golden brown. Add the apples to the pan and cook, stirring often, until they are coated with the caramelized sugar and are tender, 5 to 7 minutes. Add the butter to the pan and continue cooking the apples until the butter is melted and incorporated into the fruit. Remove the pan from heat and let the apples cool slightly.

7. Fill the center of each warm crêpe with 1/3 to 1/2 cup apple filling and a dollop of sweetened sour cream. Fold the crêpes in half, dust with confectioners' sugar, and serve immediately. Alternatively, eliminate the sour cream and serve the filled crêpes with a scoop of vanilla or caramel ice cream on the side.

The sweetest, ripest fruits of summer are quickly combined in this easy gratin.

# *R*ED *F*RUIT *G*RATIN   Serves 6 to 8

1 pound fresh sweet cherries, such as Bing cherries, pitted and halved

4 cups fresh strawberries, hulled and sliced

4 cups fresh raspberries

3 tablespoons sugar

2 tablespoons kirsch or other cherry brandy or fresh orange juice

*TOPPING:*

2 cups crème fraîche

1 teaspoon pure vanilla extract

9 tablespoons sugar

1. In a large bowl, combine the cherries, strawberries, and raspberries and toss with the 3 tablespoons sugar and the brandy or juice. Spoon the fruit into a large gratin dish or shallow heat-proof casserole.

2. To make the topping: In a small bowl, stir the crème fraîche, vanilla, and 3 tablespoons of the sugar together. Spread the mixture over the fruit in an even layer. Sprinkle with the remaining 6 tablespoons sugar.

3. Use a mini propane or butane blow-torch to caramelize the sugar on top of the cream. If you choose to caramelize the sugar under the broiler, chill the gratin for at least 1 hour and up to 3 hours until very cold. Preheat the broiler. Place the gratin under the broiler 2 inches from the heat source and cook until sugar is browned and bubbly, about 2 minutes. Serve immediately.

In the seventh grade, Miss Larson, my favorite French teacher, invited our entire small class to her home to prepare an authentic French dinner. We bravely sampled snails, sopping up the garlicky juices with French bread, and melted Gruyère cheese over our onion soup. We ended our meal with chocolate mousse and these wonderful strawberries. I loved them then, and have prepared them often ever since.

# $S$ TRAWBERRIES $G$ RAND $M$ ARNIER   Serves 6 to 8

**6 cups fresh strawberries,**
**hulled and quartered**

**¼ cup Grand Marnier or other**
**orange liqueur**

**¼ cup fresh orange juice**
**2 tablespoons superfine sugar**

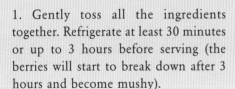

1. Gently toss all the ingredients together. Refrigerate at least 30 minutes or up to 3 hours before serving (the berries will start to break down after 3 hours and become mushy).

2. Serve the berries alone, with Crème Chantilly (page 129), over ice cream or sorbet, or alongside Coeur à la Crème (page 100).

# POACHING FRUIT

Poaching fruit—cooking it slowly in a sugar syrup—allows it to retain its natural shape and texture while making it tender and infusing it with intense flavor. Many fresh fruits are delicious poached, including pears, apples, peaches, sweet and sour cherries, figs, rhubarb, and pineapple. Dried fruits such as figs, cherries, prunes, apricots, and raisins also poach well. Poached fruit can be served warm or cold. Cooling the fruit in the poaching liquid deepens the flavor.

1. **Poach it sweet:** Poaching liquids include sugar. The sugar in the liquid not only sweetens the fruit, it slows the cooking process, which prevents the fruit from falling apart as it cooks, while becoming tender and full of flavor.

2. **Simmer it slowly:** Poaching is a slow, gentle method of cooking. Never boil the fruit. In order for the fruit to retain its shape and absorb all the flavors infused into the poaching liquid, a gentle hand and low heat are required.

3. **Intensify the flavor:** Saturate the fruit with added flavor by infusing the poaching liquid with a variety of flavoring agents such as vanilla beans; fresh ginger; citrus zest; spices such as cinnamon sticks, cloves, peppercorns, and star anise; or herbs such as rosemary, mint, and bay leaves. All or part of the water can be replaced with red wine, white wine, or champagne. Fortified wines such as port are too strong for fruits other than pears and, even with pears, they should replace no more than half the water in the poaching liquid.

**This classic French dessert is enriched by poaching the pears** in a caramelized sugar syrup spiked with fresh ginger and Poire William, a heady pear brandy. You can drizzle caramel sauce over the pears and ice cream instead of the more traditional chocolate sauce.

# *Caramel Pears Belle Hélène*   Serves 8

2-inch piece fresh ginger

1 cup sugar

3 cups warm water

1 vanilla bean, halved lengthwise

4 firm, barely ripe Bosc pears

1 or 2 tablespoons Poire William or other pear brandy (optional)

1½ pints vanilla ice cream

Chocolate Sauce (page 134) or Caramel Sauce (page 133) for serving

2 tablespoons chopped pistachios for garnish

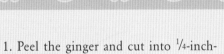

1. Peel the ginger and cut into ¼-inch-thick disks.

2. In a deep saucepan large enough to hold the pear halves in a single layer, combine the ginger, sugar, and ½ cup of the water. Bring to a boil over high heat. Cook the syrup until it turns a medium amber brown. Remove the pan from heat and carefully add the remaining 2½ cups water. Stir until the caramel is completely dissolved. Add the vanilla bean to the syrup.

3. Peel the pears, leaving the stems intact. Cut the pears in half lengthwise. Use a melon baller to remove the central core. Draw the melon baller from the core to the top of the pear, removing the interior stem, up to the top of the pear. Add the pears to the caramel syrup.

4. Simmer and cook the pears, uncovered, until they are tender but not mushy when pierced with a sharp knife, 15 to 20 minutes (the length of poaching time depends on the ripeness of the fruit). Stir in the pear brandy, if using.

5. Remove the pan from heat and let the pears cool to room temperature in the poaching liquid. The pears can be served immediately, or covered and refrigerated in the poaching liquid for up to 2 days.

6. To serve, drain the pears and place each pear half on a dessert plate. Place a scoop of vanilla ice cream alongside or on top of the poached pear. Drizzle with chocolate or caramel sauce. Sprinkle with the pistachios and serve immediately.

Caramel Pears Belle Hélène

**This creamy fresh cheese dessert is simple to prepare and requires no cooking!** Although the traditional porcelain mold makes a charming heart-shaped dessert, the cream can also be drained in a large cheesecloth-lined sieve. Simply scoop as you would ice cream, drizzle with raspberry coulis, and garnish with fresh raspberries. This coeur à la crème is light and delicately creamy, and the variation that follows is denser and more luscious. Both are delicious.

# COEUR À LA CRÈME   Serves 6

1 cup heavy cream

⅔ cup sugar

2 egg whites

1 cup (8 ounces) plain organic or low-fat natural yogurt (without any added thickeners such as carrageenan or pectin)

1 teaspoon pure vanilla extract

Raspberry Coulis (page 135)

Fresh raspberries for garnish

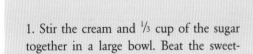

1. Stir the cream and ⅓ cup of the sugar together in a large bowl. Beat the sweetened cream until soft peaks form. Set aside.

2. In a large bowl, using an electric mixer, beat the egg whites to soft peaks. Continue beating, adding the remaining ⅓ cup sugar 1 tablespoon at a time, until the whites form stiff, glossy peaks. Fold the cream mixture and beaten egg whites into the yogurt. Fold in the vanilla.

3. Line 1 large or 6 individual coeur à la crème molds or a large sieve with a double thickness of damp cheesecloth, allowing the excess to hang over the edge.

4. Fill the prepared mold(s) with the cream mixture and set over a large plate to drain. If using a sieve, set the sieve over a bowl. Fold the excess cheesecloth over the cream. Cover with plastic wrap and refrigerate for 24 hours.

5. Unwrap and invert the mold(s) onto a serving plate or plates. Remove the cheesecloth. Or, if using the sieve, invert onto a large plate and use an ice cream scoop to spoon individual servings into dessert bowls. Surround the coeur à la crème(s) with Raspberry Coulis and a few fresh raspberries.

**VARIATION:**

In a medium bowl, using a wooden spoon, beat 8 ounces softened mascarpone cheese, ½ cup sugar, and 1 teaspoon pure vanilla extract together until smooth and creamy. In a large bowl, beat 1 cup heavy cream until it forms soft peaks. Fold the whipped cream into the mascarpone cheese mixture. Mold, drain, and serve as in the above recipe.

HOT, COLD, AND CREAMY

Coeur à la Crème

**Suave and velvety—like a swan dive into chocolate heaven—**these pots de crème are not your everyday chocolate pudding. The best thing about these sinful treats is how easy they are to make with such basic equipment.

# CHOCOLATE POTS DE CRÈME  Makes 6 custards

8 ounces semisweet or bittersweet chocolate, coarsely chopped, or semisweet chocolate morsels

2 cups heavy cream

½ cup milk

6 egg yolks

½ cup superfine sugar

2 tablespoons dark rum, Kahlúa, Grand Marnier, or Cognac

1 teaspoon pure vanilla extract

White chocolate and/or semisweet chocolate curls for garnishing

1. Place an oven rack on the middle shelf of the oven. Preheat the oven to 300°F.

2. Place the chocolate in a medium bowl.

3. In a medium saucepan, heat the cream and milk over medium-high heat until bubbles form around the edges of the pan and the milk mixture is just ready to boil. Pour over the chocolate and let sit for about 30 seconds to soften the chocolate. Stir until smooth.

4. In a medium bowl, use a large balloon whisk to beat the egg yolks together. Gradually whisk in the sugar until smooth and combined. Whisk in rum and vanilla. Gradually whisk the chocolate mixture into the egg yolks until combined.

5. Strain the custard through a fine-meshed sieve into a large container with a pouring spout. Divide the custard among 6 custard cups or ramekins. Place the cups in a 9-by-13-inch baking pan. Place the baking pan on the middle rack of the oven. Fill the pan with boiling water until it reaches halfway up the sides of the custard cups or ramekins. Cover the baking pan with aluminum foil, piercing it in several places to allow the steam to escape.

6. Bake for about 30 minutes, or until the tops of the pots de crème appear solid but the custard jiggles slightly when shaken. The perfect consistency is soft, but not liquid. The custards will firm up as they cool. Transfer the cups or ramekins from the baking pan to a wire rack and let cool to room temperature. Cover each cup with plastic wrap and refrigerate for at least 2 hours or up to 2 days before serving. Garnish the custards with semisweet chocolate and/or white chocolate curls and serve.

HOT, COLD, AND CREAMY

Chocolate Pots de Crème with Almond Tuile, *page 20*

**If you are a fan of coffee ice cream, this dense, satiny custard will send you to the moon.** Instead of using custard cups, I like to bake the mixture in coffee, espresso, or demitasse cups (check with the manufacturer to make sure the cups are ovenproof first). Set the cups on their saucers to serve.

# CAFÉ AU LAIT POTS DE CRÈME Makes 6 custards

¼ cup French or Italian roast coffee beans

2 cups heavy cream

½ cup milk

6 egg yolks

½ cup superfine sugar

1 teaspoon pure vanilla extract

Pinch of salt

Crème Chantilly (page 129) and ground cinnamon for garnish

1. Pulse the coffee beans in a coffee grinder once or twice just to crack or very coarsely grind them. Alternatively, place the coffee beans in a self-sealing plastic bag and pound with the bottom of a heavy saucepan or meat mallet to coarsely crack them.

2. In a medium saucepan, heat the cream and milk with the coffee beans over medium-high heat until bubbles form around the edges of the pan and the mixture is just ready to boil. Remove the pan from heat and cover. Let the cream steep with the coffee beans for 30 to 60 minutes.

3. Meanwhile, use a large balloon whisk to beat the egg yolks together in a medium bowl. Gradually whisk in the sugar until smooth and combined. Whisk in the vanilla and salt. Strain the cooled coffee cream through a fine-meshed sieve into the egg yolk mixture and whisk to combine. Discard coffee beans.

4. Place an oven rack on the middle shelf of the oven. Preheat oven to 300°F.

5. Strain the custard through a fine-meshed sieve into a large container with a pouring spout. Divide the custard among 6 ovenproof coffee, espresso, demitasse cups, or custard cups. Place the cups in a 9-by-13-inch baking pan. Place the baking pan on the middle rack of the oven. Fill the pan with boiling water until it reaches halfway up the sides of the coffee cups or custard cups. Cover the baking pan with aluminum foil, piercing the foil in several places for steam to escape.

6. Bake for about 40 minutes, or until the pots de crème are firm around the edges, with a slightly wobbly center about the size of a quarter. Remove the custards from the water bath and cool to room temperature on a wire rack. When cool, cover each cup with plastic wrap and refrigerate for at least 2 hours or up to 2 days before serving.

7. If using coffee, espresso, or demitasse cups, place them on saucers. Before serving, top the custards with a dollop of Crème Chantilly and dust with cinnamon.

HOT, COLD, AND CREAMY

# INFUSING LIQUIDS

Many different liquids can be infused with flavor. Water, sugar syrups, cream, and milk are the most common.

Fresh herbs such as rosemary, mint, and thyme; whole spices such as cinnamon sticks and blade mace; and other flavoring agents such as fresh ginger, citrus zest, vanilla beans, and coarsely ground coffee beans all add an intensity and depth of flavor to dishes when they are steeped, or infused, with the liquids in the recipe. Infusing extracts the elusive essence of an ingredient and imparts a more complex flavor to the recipe.

**To infuse liquid:** Combine the liquid with the flavoring agent in a saucepan. Place over medium heat, stirring occasionally. Remove the saucepan from the heat just before the liquid comes to a boil. Cover the pan and let the mixture steep until the flavor and aroma have permeated the liquid, 30 to 60 minutes. Remove the flavoring agent and proceed to use the liquid as directed in the recipe.

**Who would guess that the combination of a few simple kitchen staples** could be transformed into such an utterly delicious, indecently simple dessert? Literally "burnt cream," this devastatingly rich concoction is the undisputed queen of custards. It's so easy to conjure up you'll prepare it for every dinner party until your friends scream for mercy. One caveat: With such a supremely simple dessert, it is necessary to use vanilla beans of good quality—no substitutions. Luckily, most large grocery stores with a decent spice or baking section carry them. If you invest in one of the newly popular mini blowtorches made especially for the home cook (most kitchenware stores carry them), making the crackled sugar topping is easy. Feel like a true pastry chef and demonstrate it for your guests, or let them take turns caramelizing their own custard as part of the fun.

# CRÈME BRÛLÉE    Makes 6 custards

2 cups heavy cream

1 or 2 vanilla beans

6 egg yolks

½ cup superfine sugar

1 teaspoon pure vanilla extract

Pinch of salt

¼ cup granulated sugar for topping

1. Pour the cream into a heavy saucepan. Split the vanilla bean(s) lengthwise with the tip of a sharp paring knife. Use the tip of the knife to carefully scrape the sticky black seeds from inside the pod. Add the seeds and the pod to the cream. Don't worry if the seeds seem to float in the cream in little globs; you will separate them later.

2. Heat the cream over medium heat until bubbles form around the edges of the pan. Just before the cream comes to a boil, remove the pan from heat and cover. Allow the cream to steep with the vanilla for 1 hour.

3. Place an oven rack on the middle shelf of the oven. Preheat the oven to 325°F.

4. In a medium bowl, whisk the egg yolks together. Gradually add the superfine sugar to the yolks, whisking constantly, until smooth and combined.

5. Remove the vanilla bean pods from the cream. Gradually whisk the cooled cream into the egg yolks, breaking up any little clumps of black seeds as you do so. Whisk in salt and vanilla extract.

6. Strain the custard through a fine-meshed sieve into a container with a pouring spout. Divide the custard mixture among 6 custard cups or individual ramekins. Place the cups in a 9-by-13-inch baking pan. Place the baking pan on the middle rack of the preheated oven. Fill the pan with boiling water until it reaches halfway up the sides of the custard cups or ramekins. Cover the pan with aluminum foil, piercing the foil in several places for steam to escape.

7. Bake for about 40 minutes, or until the custards are firm around the edges with a slightly wobbly center about the size of a quarter. Remove the custards from the water bath and let them cool to room temperature on a wire rack. Cover each cup with plastic wrap and refrigerate at least 3 hours and up to 2 days.

8. Right before serving, sprinkle each custard with 2 teaspoons granulated sugar in a thin, even layer. Use a mini blowtorch to caramelize the sugar. Or, preheat the broiler, and place the custards in a baking pan filled with ice cubes and cold water (see sidebar). Place the custards about 2 inches from the heat source and broil for 2 minutes, or until the sugar caramelizes.

## CARAMELIZING A SUGAR TOPPING

There are two ways to create the famous crackled sugar topping on a crème brûlée.

The blowtorch: The easiest and most fun method for caramelizing the sugar topping on a crème brûlée is with a blowtorch. Propane-powered blowtorches are widely available in most hardware stores, and smaller butane-powered versions created especially for the home cook are available in many kitchenware shops.

To caramelize: Sprinkle 2 teaspoons sugar in a thin layer over the top of each chilled custard. Ignite the blowtorch and hold the flame about 2 inches from the top of a custard. Move the flame over the sugar until it melts and begins to turn brown, about 1 minute. As the sugar browns, it will form a glossy, crisp, wafer-thin layer on top of the custard.

The broiler: If you don't have a blowtorch, or find the method intimidating, you can caramelize the sugar under a very hot broiler. Fill a large baking or roasting pan with ice cubes. Nestle the chilled custards in the ice and fill the pan with cold water so the molds are surrounded with ice water. Do not attempt to caramelize the sugar without the benefit of this ice water bath—the cold custard will melt into an unappetizing goo if you do.

To caramelize: Sprinkle 2 teaspoons sugar in a thin layer over the top of each custard. Place the custards about 2 inches from the heat source and broil for 1 to 2 minutes, or until the sugar has caramelized. Watch carefully; it may be necessary to turn the pan to evenly brown the sugar on all the custards. Remove the pan from the oven.

Note: Crème brûlée can be refrigerated for 15 to 30 minutes before the sugar begins to soften.

**Sugar, eggs, milk, and cream are transformed** into this delicious caramel sauce–glazed confection. The definitive French custard, crème caramel balances a luscious, creamy flavor with a quivering, melt-in-your-mouth texture–the perfect finale to any meal.

# CRÈME CARAMEL  Makes one 8-inch or 6 individual custards

**CARAMEL:**

1 cup sugar

2 tablespoons water

½ teaspoon fresh lemon juice

**CUSTARD:**

2 large eggs

4 egg yolks

½ cup sugar

1 tablespoon pure vanilla extract

Pinch of salt

1½ cups heavy cream

1½ cups milk

1. To make the caramel: If using individual molds, fill a large bowl with ice water and set it on the counter next to the stove. Combine the sugar, water, and lemon juice in a medium saucepan and cook over medium heat, swirling the pan occasionally, until the sugar dissolves and starts to turn color. Increase heat to high and let the mixture bubble until it turns a rich caramel brown, swirling the pan occasionally to make sure the sugar browns evenly. This should take about 4 to 5 minutes. If the mixture gets too brown–about the color of a dirty penny–it will start to smoke and the resulting caramel will taste burned.

2. If using the individual molds, remove the caramel from heat and dip the bottom of the pan in the bowl of ice water. This will stop the cooking process and keep the caramel from overcooking while you are coating the molds. Pour about 2 tablespoons caramel into each of six 6-ounce custard cups or ramekins. If the caramel gets a little too thick to pour towards the end, warm it gently over low heat. Or, pour the caramel directly into an 8-inch straight-sided cake pan and swirl to coat the bottom completely with caramel. Set aside.

3. Place an oven rack on the middle shelf of the oven. Preheat the oven to 325°F.

4. To make the custard: In a medium bowl, whisk the eggs, yolks, sugar, vanilla, and salt together until smooth and combined.

RECIPE CONTINUES >>

Crème Caramel

5. Stir the cream and milk together in a large saucepan over medium heat until bubbles form around the edge of the pan and the milk mixture is just about to boil. Remove from heat and slowly whisk 1 cup of the hot milk mixture into the eggs. Gradually whisk the remaining milk mixture into the eggs, 1 cup at a time.

6. Strain the custard through a fine-meshed sieve into a container with a pouring spout. Divide the custard mixture among the prepared cups or ramekins or pour into the cake pan. Place the mold(s) in a 9-by-13-inch baking pan. Place the pan on the oven rack.

Fill the pan with boiling water to reach halfway up the sides of the mold(s). Cover the baking pan with aluminum foil, piercing the foil in several places for steam to escape. Bake the individual custards for 40 to 45 minutes or the larger custard for 70 to 80 minutes, or until a knife inserted into the center of the custard comes out clean.

7. Transfer the custard(s) from the water bath to a wire rack and let cool completely at room temperature. When completely cool, cover with plastic wrap and refrigerate for at least 3 hours or up to 2 days.

8. To unmold, run a table knife around the perimeter of the custard, pressing it against the side of the mold to loosen it, but avoiding cutting into the custard. Hold a serving plate over the top of the custard and invert. Shake the mold gently to release the custard. Remove the mold, and let the caramel sauce flow down the sides of the custard. Serve immediately.

## MAKING CARAMEL

Just as Rumpelstiltskin spun humble straw into gold, simple sugar can be transformed, with the application of a little heat, into caramel: a translucent, liquid gold essence with a complex and distinctive flavor. Liquid caramel can be used to line custard molds, combined with cream to form a luscious sauce, twirled into golden spun sugar, or cooled to form a brittle amber candy.

The classic French pan for melting sugar is an untinned copper saucepan with a pouring spout built into the lip, called a sugar pot. A heavy stainless steel–lined pan or a heavy aluminum pan can also be used with success.

**Dry method:** Sugar is placed in the pan, then cooked and stirred constantly over low heat until it melts and turns a deep amber-red color. Although the color is startlingly beautiful, caramel created from dry sugar cooks very fast and is easy to burn. Even with constant stirring, hard granules of sugar can develop when bits of the sugar don't melt uniformly, and it is almost impossible to get these granules to melt before the rest of the caramel overcooks and burns.

**Wet method:** Sugar is mixed with a little water until it forms a sandy paste. A little lemon juice or cream of tartar can be added to prevent recrystallization of any of the sugar crystals. The sugar is allowed to dissolve completely undisturbed, over medium heat. Once it comes to a boil, it isn't stirred, but merely swirled in the pan to ensure even browning. This method is easier than the dry method.

## THE WATER BATH

Many dishes, notably custards, savory mousses, and pâtés, benefit from being baked in a water bath or *bain marie*. The dish containing the custard or mousse is set in a larger pan (such as a baking or roasting pan) of hot water and transferred to the oven. The water absorbs the harsh, direct heat of the oven, keeping the cooking slow and even. Baking custards slowly in a water bath guarantees a silky-smooth, rather than a rubbery, texture.

Chocolate mousse is the quintessential French dessert, versatile as a component in more elaborate cakes and pastries, yet perfect served alone with just a dollop of whipped cream. I've included two versions of this classic. The first, lightened only with beaten egg whites, is heavier and denser, with an intense, buttery chocolate flavor. The second version incorporates whipped cream to mellow the flavor of the chocolate and provide a smooth, velvety texture.

# CHOCOLATE MOUSSE TWO WAYS
## CHOCOLATE MOUSSE NUMBER 1

6 ounces semisweet chocolate, coarsely chopped, or semisweet chocolate morsels

½ cup (1 stick) unsalted butter, cut into 8 pieces

4 large egg yolks

4 tablespoons sugar

1 or 2 tablespoons Cognac, dark rum, Grand Marnier, or whiskey

2 teaspoons instant coffee or espresso dissolved in 2 teaspoons hot water

1 teaspoon pure vanilla extract

3 egg whites

⅛ teaspoon cream of tartar

1. In a double boiler over barely simmering water, melt the chocolate with the butter. Stir until smooth. Or, combine the chocolate and the butter in a microwave-safe bowl and microwave on medium for 1½ to 4 minutes, or until the butter melts and chocolate becomes shiny but still maintains its shape. Remove the container from the microwave and stir the chocolate and butter together until smooth.

2. In a large bowl, using a hand-held mixer set at medium speed, beat the egg yolks until blended. Gradually add 2 tablespoons of the sugar and beat for 4 to 6 minutes, or until the yolks turn pale yellow and form a slowly dissolving ribbon on the surface of the mixture when the beaters are lifted. Beat in the liqueur, coffee mixture, and vanilla.

3. Using a rubber spatula, fold the melted chocolate into the beaten egg yolks just until combined.

4. In a large bowl, beat the egg whites and cream of tartar with an electric mixer at low speed until foamy. Increase the mixer speed to medium-high and continue beating until soft peaks form. Continue beating, gradually adding the remaining 2 tablespoons sugar, until stiff, glossy peaks form.

5. Stir one third of the beaten egg whites into the chocolate mixture to lighten it. Using a rubber spatula, fold in the remaining whites just until incorporated. Spoon the mousse into 8 individual serving dishes or into 1 large bowl. Cover lightly with plastic wrap and refrigerate at least 4 hours or up to 2 days.

# CHOCOLATE MOUSSE NUMBER 2

8 ounces semisweet or bittersweet chocolate, coarsely chopped, or semisweet chocolate morsels

¼ cup brewed coffee

2 large eggs, separated

4 tablespoons sugar

1 teaspoon pure vanilla extract

2 tablespoons dark rum, Cognac, Grand Marnier, or whiskey (optional)

Pinch of cream of tartar

1 cup heavy cream

1. Combine the chocolate and coffee in a small saucepan. Melt the chocolate over low heat, stirring constantly, until smooth. Remove from heat.

2. In a medium bowl, using a hand-held mixer set at medium speed, beat the egg yolks until blended. Gradually add 2 tablespoons of the sugar and beat for 4 to 6 minutes, or until the yolks turn pale yellow and form a slowly dissolving ribbon on the surface of the mixture when the beaters are lifted. Beat in the vanilla and rum, Cognac, Grand Marnier, or whiskey (if using).

3. Using a large rubber spatula, fold the melted chocolate into the beaten egg yolks until combined.

4. In a large bowl, beat the egg whites and cream of tartar with an electric mixer on low speed until foamy. Increase the mixer speed to medium-high and continue beating until soft peaks form. Continue beating, gradually adding the remaining 2 tablespoons sugar, until stiff, glossy peaks form.

5. Stir one third of the beaten whites into the chocolate mixture to lighten it. Spoon the remaining beaten whites on top of the chocolate mixture without folding them in.

6. In a large bowl, using an electric mixer, beat the cream until it forms soft peaks. Using a large rubber spatula, fold the cream and the remaining beaten egg whites into chocolate mixture just until combined. Spoon the mousse into 8 individual serving dishes or into 1 large bowl. Cover lightly with plastic wrap and refrigerate for at least 4 hours or up to 2 days.

**Although there are delicious, high-quality commercial ice creams available,** somehow nothing equals fresh homemade ice cream. And with homemade ice cream, you can create unusual, distinctive flavors unavailable anywhere except your own kitchen. This classic French vanilla ice cream is a good place to begin.

# French Vanilla Ice Cream   Makes 1½ quarts

1 vanilla bean

2 cups whole milk

2 cups heavy cream

6 egg yolks, beaten

1 cup sugar

Pinch of salt

2 teaspoons vanilla extract

1. Using the tip of a sharp paring knife, slice the vanilla bean in half lengthwise. Use the back of the knife to carefully scrape the sticky vanilla seeds from the pod. Combine the milk and cream in a medium saucepan. Add the seeds and the pod to the milk and cream. The seeds will stick together in little globs; use a whisk to vigorously disperse them through the mixture.

2. Heat the milk mixture over medium heat until small bubbles begin to form around the edges of the pan and it is just about to boil. Remove from heat and cover. Let the milk mixture infuse for 30 minutes to 1 hour. Remove the vanilla bean from the pan, but do not strain; you want to keep the little black vanilla seeds in the final custard.

3. In a large bowl, whisk the egg yolks, sugar, and salt together until smooth. Slowly whisk the cooled milk mixture into the yolks. Return the mixture back to the saucepan.

4. Cook the custard, stirring it constantly over low heat, until it thickens enough to coat the back of the spoon; your finger should leave a clear line through the custard when drawn down the back of the spoon. (Be very careful not to allow the custard to get too hot, or even close to boiling; the custard will curdle and separate if it does.) Immediately remove the custard from heat and quickly strain it through a fine-meshed sieve into a bowl. Stir in the vanilla extract.

5. Place the bowl of custard over a larger bowl filled with ice and water, and let cool, stirring occasionally. When cool, remove the bowl from the ice water and cover with plastic wrap, pressing it into the surface of the custard to prevent a skin from forming. Refrigerate for at least 4 hours or preferably overnight. The custard must be completely cold before being frozen in an ice cream maker.

6. Freeze the custard in an ice cream maker according to the manufacturer's instructions. Store the ice cream in a resealable plastic or stainless steel container in the freezer until ready to serve. Ice cream is best served within a few hours of being made.

**VARIATION:** *Fresh Mint Ice Cream*

Coarsely rip 1 cup packed fresh mint leaves to bruise them and release their flavor. Add to the milk mixture in place of the vanilla bean at the beginning of step 2 of the French Vanilla Ice Cream recipe (page 115). Heat, cover, and let infuse for 30 minutes to 1 hour. Remove the mint leaves after infusing the milk mixture and proceed as in the above recipe, omitting the vanilla extract.

# INGREDIENTS FOR PERFECT ICE CREAM

**Milk and cream:** The perfect ice cream combines both milk and cream. The protein in the milk and the butterfat in the cream work in combination as the mixture freezes to keep the ice crystals small, ensuring a creamy texture. The cream holds air as it freezes, yielding a smooth, dense texture. Milk cuts the butterfat in the cream, preventing the mixture from being too stiff or greasy. If there is too much cream, the ice cream will have a sandy or grainy texture. Too much milk in the mixture, and the ice cream will be too icy. The right combination of milk and cream yields an ice cream that is light, smooth, and creamy.

**Eggs:** Egg yolks add richness without butterfat. They also act as a stabilizer and an emulsifier in custard, preventing the milk and cream from separating.

**Heating the custard:** In French-custard ice creams, it is necessary to heat the mixture to cook the egg yolks and thicken the mixture. Custard-based ice creams are especially creamy and smooth without being overly rich.

**Chilling the custard:** Chilling allows flavors to mellow and blend, maximizing the intensity of flavor in your ice cream. Chilling also gives the finished ice cream more body and a denser texture.

**Adding alcohol:** Spirits such as Cognac, dark rum, whiskey, liqueurs, and even vanilla extract add flavor and reduce the freezing point of ice cream, making it easier to scoop. Too much alcohol, however, will keep the ice cream from freezing properly and it will be mushy. A good rule of thumb is 1 tablespoon alcohol per 2 cups (1 pint) of ice cream mixture.

**The rich, complex flavor of caramel elevates this ice cream to new heights.** It is wonderful alone or alongside apple, pear, or chocolate desserts.

# CARAMEL ICE CREAM

Makes 1 quart

**CARAMEL:**

1 cup sugar

2 tablespoons water

¼ teaspoon fresh lemon juice

**CUSTARD:**

2 cups heavy cream

1½ cups milk

6 egg yolks

⅛ teaspoon salt

2 teaspoons pure vanilla extract

1. To make the caramel: Combine the sugar, water, and lemon juice in a medium saucepan and cook over medium heat, swirling the pan occasionally, until the sugar dissolves and starts to turn color. Increase the heat to high and let the mixture bubble until it turns a rich caramel brown, swirling the pan occasionally to make sure the sugar browns evenly. This should take about 4 to 5 minutes. (If the mixture gets too brown—about the color of a dirty penny—it will start to smoke and the resulting caramel will taste burned.)

2. Remove the pan from heat and carefully stir in the cream with a long-handled wooden spoon until smooth. Be careful, as the hot caramel will hiss and spit as the cold cream hits it. Stir in the milk.

3. In a medium bowl, whisk the egg yolks and salt until smooth. Whisk ¼ cup of the hot caramel mixture into the yolks. Gradually whisk the remaining caramel mixture into the yolks, ¼ cup at a time, until completely combined. Return the mixture to the saucepan.

4. Cook the custard over very low heat, stirring constantly, until it thickens enough to coat the back of the spoon; your finger will leave a clear line through the custard when drawn down the back of the spoon. Be very careful not to allow the custard to get too hot, or even close to boiling; the custard will curdle and separate if it does. Immediately remove the custard from the heat and quickly strain it through a fine-meshed sieve into a bowl. Stir in the vanilla extract.

5. Place the bowl of custard over a larger bowl filled with ice water and let cool, stirring occasionally. Remove the bowl from ice water and cover with plastic wrap, pressing it onto the surface of the custard to prevent a skin from forming. Refrigerate for at least 4 hours or preferably overnight. The custard must be completely cold before freezing in an ice cream maker.

6. Freeze the custard in an ice cream maker according to the manufacturer's instructions. Store in a resealable plastic or stainless steel container in the freezer until ready to serve. Ice cream is best served within a few hours of being made.

Ice Cream

**At Ma Bourgogne, in the beautiful Place des Vosges in Paris,** I ordered this fancifully named ice cream unsure of what I would get. I was delighted to dip my spoon into a rich coffee ice cream chockful of toasted walnuts. The Dauphine region of France extends from Savoy to Provence and is known for its walnuts—which may be how this particular ice cream got its name.

# Mocha Dauphinois Ice Cream 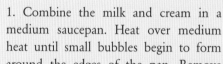 Makes 1½ quarts

2 cups milk

2 cups heavy cream

2 tablespoons instant coffee or espresso powder dissolved in 2 teaspoons hot water

6 egg yolks, beaten

1 cup sugar

Pinch of salt

2 teaspoons pure vanilla extract

¾ to 1 cup walnuts, toasted and coarsely chopped (see page 19)

1. Combine the milk and cream in a medium saucepan. Heat over medium heat until small bubbles begin to form around the edges of the pan. Remove from the heat and stir in the coffee mixture.

2. In a medium bowl, whisk the egg yolks, sugar, and salt together until smooth. Whisk ¼ cup of the hot milk mixture into the yolks. Gradually whisk the remaining milk mixture into the yolks, ¼ cup at a time, until completely combined. Return the mixture to the saucepan.

3. Cook the custard, stirring it constantly over very low heat, until it thickens enough to coat the back of the spoon; your finger will leave a clear line through the custard when drawn down the back of the spoon. Be very careful not to allow the custard to get too hot, or even close to boiling; it will curdle and separate if it does. Immediately remove the custard from heat and quickly strain it through a fine-meshed sieve into a medium bowl. Stir in the vanilla extract.

4. Place the bowl of custard over a larger bowl filled with ice water and let cool, stirring occasionally. Remove the bowl from ice water and cover it with plastic wrap, pressing it onto the surface of the custard to prevent a skin from forming.

Refrigerate for at least 4 hours or preferably overnight. The custard must be completely cold before freezing in an ice cream maker.

5. Freeze the custard in an ice cream maker according to the manufacturer's instructions. When the ice cream is thickened but not completely frozen, about 8 to 10 minutes into the freezing process, stop the ice cream maker and add the toasted walnuts to the ice cream. Continue freezing until firm. Store the ice cream in a resealable plastic or stainless steel container in the freezer until ready to serve. Ice cream is best served within a few hours of being made.

**Berthillon, nestled in an idyllic location on the peaceful and charming Ile St-Louis,** makes the best ice cream and sorbet in Paris. Their mind-boggling variety of more than fifty enticing flavors includes *chocolat noir, kumquat, nougat glace, cocktail exotique,* and this delicious and invigorating *créole*–or rum raisin–ice cream.

# CRÉOLE ICE CREAM Makes 1½ quarts

| | | |
|---|---|---|
| ¼ cup dark raisins | 2 cups whole milk | ¾ cup sugar |
| ¼ cup golden raisins | 2 cups heavy cream | Pinch of salt |
| 6 tablespoons dark rum | 6 egg yolks | 1 teaspoon pure vanilla extract |

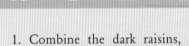

HOT, COLD, AND CREAMY

1. Combine the dark raisins, golden raisins, and dark rum in a medium saucepan. Warm over medium heat but do not boil. Remove from heat and let the raisins steep for at least 30 minutes.

2. Combine the milk and cream in a medium saucepan. Heat over medium heat until bubbles begin to form around the edges of the pan and the mixture is just about to boil. Remove the pan from heat.

3. In a medium bowl, whisk the egg yolks, sugar, and salt together until smooth. Drain the rum from the raisins and whisk it into the egg yolks. Reserve raisins. Whisk ¼ cup of the hot milk mixture into the yolks. Continue whisking the milk mixture into the yolks, ¼ cup at a time, until completely combined. Return the mixture to the saucepan.

4. Cook the custard, stirring it constantly over very low heat, until it thickens enough to coat the back of the spoon; your finger will leave a clear line through the custard when drawn down the back of the spoon. Be very careful not to allow the custard to get too hot, or even close to boiling; it will curdle and separate if it does. Immediately remove the custard from heat and quickly strain it through a fine-meshed sieve into a medium bowl. Stir in the vanilla extract.

5. Place the bowl of custard over a larger bowl filled with ice water and let cool, stirring occasionally. Remove the bowl from ice water and cover with plastic wrap, pressing it onto the surface of the custard to prevent a skin from forming. Refrigerate for at least 4 hours or preferably overnight. The custard must be completely cold before freezing in an ice cream maker.

6. Freeze the custard in an ice cream maker according to the manufacturer's instructions. When the ice cream is thickened but not completely frozen, about 8 to 10 minutes into the freezing process, stop the ice cream maker and add the rum-soaked raisins to the ice cream. Continue freezing until firm. Store the ice cream in a resealable plastic or stainless steel container in the freezer until ready to serve. Ice cream is best served within a few hours of being made.

A vibrant, fresh-tasting sorbet flavored with crème de cassis, a liqueur derived from black currants.

# BLACKBERRY CASSIS SORBET   Makes 1½ pints

1 pound frozen unsweetened
blackberries, thawed

2 tablespoons fresh lemon juice

1 cup water

1 cup sugar

2 tablespoons cassis liqueur

1. Place the thawed berries and any accumulated juice in a blender or food processor and puree until smooth. Using the back of a large spoon, press the pureed berries through a fine-meshed sieve held over a bowl; discard the seeds. You should have 2 cups blackberry puree. Stir the lemon juice into the puree.

2. Combine the water and sugar in a small saucepan. Place over medium heat and bring to a boil. Cook until the sugar dissolves. Reduce the heat to medium-low and simmer for about 5 minutes, or until thickened. Remove the pan from heat and let the syrup cool completely.

3. Combine the blackberry puree, sugar syrup, and crème de cassis. Cover and refrigerate for at least 4 hours or preferably overnight.

4. Place the chilled berry mixture in an ice cream maker and freeze according to the manufacturer's instructions. Store in a resealable plastic or stainless steel container. Sorbet is best served the day it is made.

sorbet

**I tasted this unusual, deliciously tart, pale pink sorbet** during a spring trip to Paris at Berthillon, the famous ice cream spot on the Ile St-Louis, where seasonal fruits are often incorporated into their large, rotating list of ice creams and sorbets.

# RHUBARB SORBET Makes 1½ pints

**2 pounds rhubarb, cut into 1-inch pieces**

**1¼ cups water**

**1 cup sugar**

1. Combine the rhubarb and ¼ cup of the water in a medium saucepan. Cover and bring to a boil over medium-high heat. Reduce heat to medium-low and simmer the rhubarb until it is very soft and falling apart, about 5 minutes. Remove from heat and let cool slightly.

2. Puree the rhubarb in a blender or food processor until very smooth. You should have 2 cups puree. Set aside.

3. Combine the remaining 1 cup water and the sugar in a small saucepan. Place over medium heat and bring to a boil. Cook, stirring occasionally, until the sugar dissolves. Reduce heat to medium-low and simmer for about 5 minutes to thicken the sugar syrup. Remove the pan from heat and let the syrup cool to room temperature. Combine the sugar syrup and pureed rhubarb and refrigerate for at least 4 hours or preferably overnight.

4. Place the chilled rhubarb mixture in an ice cream maker and freeze according to the manufacturer's instructions. Store in a resealable plastic or stainless steel container. Sorbet is best served the day it is made.

# Building Blocks

# 4

FROM CRÈME FRAÎCHE TO BUTTERCREAM, the basics in this chapter are creative building blocks helpful in preparing and embellishing the desserts in the rest of this volume. Many of these components can be made in advance and stored in the refrigerator or freezer, always at the ready. When your kitchen is stocked with these delicious ingredients, you won't have to think twice before whipping up a simple French dessert for your family and friends.

**The perfect crème anglaise, or English cream, is thick, smooth, and velvety.** It is the basis for many great Bavarian custards and ice creams, and is the perfect complement for desserts such as Fallen Chocolate Soufflé Cake (page 78). The most important rules to remember are (1) never stop stirring; and (2) never let it boil. Straining the sauce after it is cooked will make it silky smooth.

# CRÈME ANGLAISE   Makes 3 cups

1 vanilla bean

2 cups milk

5 large egg yolks

½ cup sugar

pinch of salt

1. Using the tip of a sharp knife, slice the vanilla bean in half lengthwise. Use the back of the knife to carefully scrape the sticky seeds from the pod. Pour the milk into a medium saucepan. Add the vanilla seeds and pod to the milk. The seeds will stick together in little globs; use a whisk to vigorously disperse them through the milk.

2. Heat the milk over medium heat until small bubbles begin to form around the edges of the pan and the milk is just about to boil. Remove the pan from heat and cover. Let the milk and vanilla bean infuse together for 30 minutes to 1 hour. Remove the vanilla

pod from the pan, but do not strain; you want to keep the little black vanilla seeds in the final sauce.

3. In a medium bowl, whisk the egg yolks, sugar and salt together until smooth. Whisk ¼ cup of the milk mixture into the yolks. Gradually whisk the remaining milk mixture into the yolks, ¼ cup at a time, until completely combined. Return the mixture to the saucepan.

4. Cook the custard, stirring it constantly over very low heat, until it thickens enough to coat the back of the spoon; your finger will leave a clear line through the custard when drawn

down the back of the spoon. Be very careful not to allow the custard to get too hot, or even close to boiling; it will curdle and separate if it does. Immediately remove the custard from heat and quickly strain it through a fine-meshed sieve into a medium bowl.

5. Let the custard sauce cool for 10 minutes, stirring it occasionally to hasten cooling. Cover the surface of the custard with plastic wrap, pressing it onto the surface and piercing it in a few places with the tip of a sharp knife to allow any steam to escape. Refrigerate for at least 3 hours or up to 2 days.

# TEMPERING EGGS

Tempering is an important technique in preparing smooth, silky custards. It is the gradual addition of hot milk and/or cream to raw eggs which gradually raises the temperature of the eggs and prevents them from curdling. Combining raw eggs with a large amount of very hot liquid will "scramble" the eggs and prevent a custard from setting properly as it cooks.

To temper, add about $\frac{1}{4}$ cup hot liquid to eggs while whisking. Continue whisking hot liquid into the eggs, $\frac{1}{4}$ cup at a time, until all the liquid is incorporated.

**So easy, yet so delectable.** The only tip I can give you for this is whisk! whisk! whisk! Once this cream is set over heat, you need to whisk it quickly and constantly to prevent it from lumping. The cornstarch in this recipe not only helps thicken the cream, it allows you to cook it at a higher temperature without curdling the eggs. Pastry cream, or *crème pâtissière*, is quick, delicious, and supremely versatile.

# PASTRY CREAM   Makes 3 cups

2 cups milk

½ cup sugar

¼ cup cornstarch

2 large eggs

1 egg yolk

2 tablespoons unsalted butter

2 teaspoons pure vanilla extract

¾ cup heavy cream

1. Combine 1½ cups of the milk with the sugar in a medium, heavy saucepan.

2. In a medium bowl, dissolve the cornstarch in the remaining ½ cup milk. Whisk the eggs and yolk into the dissolved cornstarch until completely smooth.

3. Bring the milk and sugar to a boil over high heat, stirring constantly. Stir ¼ cup of the hot milk mixture into the egg mixture to temper it. Whisk in the remaining milk mixture, ¼ cup at a time until completely combined.

4. Return the mixture to the saucepan and cook over medium-high heat until the custard thickens and comes to a slow boil.

Cook, stirring constantly, for about 2 minutes. Remove the pan from the heat and stir in the butter and vanilla until both are completely incorporated.

5. Pour the custard through a fine-meshed sieve into a large bowl. Press plastic wrap over the surface of the hot pastry cream to prevent a skin from forming as the cream cools. Poke a few holes in the plastic wrap to allow steam to escape. Let the custard cool on a wire rack for 10 minutes, then refrigerate until completely cold, about 3 hours, or up to 24 hours.

6. In a large bowl, beat the cream until it forms stiff peaks. Fold one third of the whipped cream into the chilled pastry cream to soften it, then fold in the rest of the whipped cream. Use immediately, or cover and refrigerate for up to 2 days.

### VARIATION: Coffee Pastry Cream

Dissolve 2 tablespoons instant coffee or espresso powder in 1 tablespoon hot water to form a paste. Stir into the milk in the above recipe and proceed as above.

**Thick and tangy, crème fraîche has a flavor similar to sour cream.** Unlike sour cream, however, crème fraîche can be beaten, like heavy cream, and it can be heated without separating, curdling, or becoming grainy.

# CRÈME FRAÎCHE   Makes 2 cups

**2 cups heavy cream**

**2 tablespoons buttermilk**

1. Combine the heavy cream and buttermilk in a glass jar with a screw top. Cover tightly and shake to combine.

2. Let the cream stand at room temperature for 24 hours to thicken.

3. Store in the refrigerator for up to 1 week. The crème fraîche will become tangier and thicker the longer it is stored.

**This simple sweetened whipped cream, flavored with vanilla, is a perfect foil for many desserts.** Chilling the mixing bowl and beaters in the freezer for 15 minutes shortens the amount of time it takes to whip the cream.

# CRÈME CHANTILLY   Makes 4 cups

**2 cups heavy cream, preferably not ultrapasteurized**

**5 tablespoons superfine or granulated sugar**

**2 teaspoons pure vanilla extract**

1. Place a large bowl and mixer beaters in the freezer for 15 minutes. Combine all the ingredients in the bowl and beat with an electric mixer at medium-low speed until the cream starts to thicken.

2. Increase the mixer speed to medium and continue beating until the cream nearly doubles in volume and forms soft peaks. Using a large balloon whisk, finish beating the cream by hand until it forms stiff peaks.

# PERFECT WHIPPED CREAM

The proper technique for whipping cream can be confusing; the following tips should help.

**Soft peaks:** Cream is at the "soft peak" stage when it is whipped thick enough to form well-defined peaks that very slowly droop over themselves when the beaters are lifted. It will be thick, with lots of body. Cream whipped to soft peaks is the perfect texture for folding into mousses and other dishes. It is soft enough to combine easily with the other ingredients, but firm enough to add heft and body to the dish. The act of folding the cream into other ingredients will further stiffen the cream; if beaten to stiff peaks before folding, the cream will become grainy, and the dish—such as a mousse—will be coarse and grainy instead of voluptuous and creamy. Lightly sweetened cream beaten to soft peaks is also delicious served as an accompaniment to warm desserts such as a fallen chocolate soufflé cake. It is usually spooned casually over, or alongside, the dessert.

**Stiff peaks:** Cream is at the "stiff peak" stage when it forms peaks that stand firmly upright when the beaters are lifted. Cream whipped to stiff peaks is the perfect consistency for piping. It is stiff enough to hold a decorative design and can be used to garnish a cake or fill cream puffs. But be careful; it is very easy to go from stiff peaks to grainy and lumpy, where the cream starts to separate into thick curds and begins its journey towards becoming butter. To avoid this, use an electric mixer to whip the cream to soft peaks, then use a large balloon whisk to finish whipping the cream by hand to form stiff peaks—it usually takes only a few twists of the wrist to coax the cream to the texture you desire.

**I love ganache!** This thick, rich, luscious cream transports chocolate to new heights. A snap to make, it can be thrown together in minutes. Ganache has many magical incarnations. Use it to frost a cake, roll into truffles, or sandwich together macaroons or meringues. Warm ganache can be poured into a simple pastry shell to form a devastatingly elegant tart, spread over a cake for a shiny glaze, or dribbled from a spoon for a luxurious dessert sauce.

# CHOCOLATE GANACHE    Makes 2 cups

**1 pound semisweet or bittersweet chocolate, coarsely chopped, or semisweet chocolate morsels**

**1 cup heavy cream**

**2 tablespoons sugar**

**2 tablespoons unsalted butter**

**1 or 2 tablespoons dark rum, brandy, Kahlúa, Grand Marnier or other orange liqueur**

**1 teaspoon pure vanilla extract**

1. Put the chocolate in a large bowl.

2. Combine the cream, sugar, and butter in a small saucepan. Place over medium heat and stir constantly until the butter melts. Heat until bubbles start to form around the edges of the pan and the cream is just about to boil.

3. Immediately pour the hot cream over the chocolate. Let the mixture sit for 30 seconds to soften the chocolate. Stir gently until smooth and thick. Stir in the rum or other spirits, and the vanilla. While the ganache is warm and liquid, use as a dessert sauce or as a glaze for a cake. Or, chill the ganache for 30 minutes, or until firm. Chilled ganache can be formed into bite-sized truffles, or used as a filling to sandwich macaroons, meringues, or other cookies.

**Note:** To return chilled ganache to its liquid state, reheat in a double boiler over barely simmering water, stirring occasionally until melted. Or, place ganache in a microwave-safe bowl and microwave on medium heat for $1\frac{1}{2}$ to 2 minutes, until melted. Ganache can be refrigerated for up to 1 week.

BUILDING BLOCKS

**Swiss meringue buttercream is very sturdy, yet remarkably silky and creamy.** It spreads and pipes beautifully, and if you are preparing any of the other desserts in this book that require egg yolks alone, such as Crème Brûlée (page 106), Chocolate Pots de Crème (page 102), or Crème Anglaise (page 126), this is a great way to use up all those egg whites! The easiest of the French buttercreams, Swiss meringue buttercream does take time, but it is supremely easy if you have the right equipment—in this case a free-standing mixer. You can prepare it with a hand mixer, but the time required to beat it is formidable. But if you are feeling ambitious, please try it! Make sure you use softened unsalted butter and add it a little at a time.

# $S$WISS $M$ERINGUE $B$UTTERCREAM   Makes about 4 cups

10 egg whites

1½ cups sugar

1½ pounds (6 sticks) cold, unsalted butter

Flavoring of choice (see following page)

1. Combine the egg whites and sugar in the large metal bowl of a free-standing mixer.

2. Fill a large sauté pan or skillet half full with water and set over medium heat.

3. Heat the water until it simmers. Place the bowl in the simmering water and whisk the egg whites and sugar constantly until the sugar is dissolved and the whites are hot to the touch (about 120°F), 3 to 4 minutes.

4. Remove the bowl from heat and, using the whisk attachment, beat the egg whites at medium-high speed until they are completely cool, doubled in volume, and form stiff, glossy peaks (about 10 minutes); check to make sure the bottom of the bowl is completely cool to the touch before adding the butter.

5. While the meringue is being beaten, prepare the butter: Unwrap the butter and rewrap the sticks loosely in a sheet of plastic wrap. Pound the butter 5 or 6 times with a rolling pin, or until the butter is soft and malleable but is still cold.

6. With the mixer speed on medium, add the butter about 2 tablespoons at a time and beat in each addition until it is incorporated into the meringue. When all the butter has been incorporated, stop the mixer and stir in the flavorings by hand. The buttercream can be used immediately, covered and refrigerated for up to 1 week, or frozen for up to 1 month.

7. Cold or frozen buttercream needs to thaw completely and come to room temperature before being beaten again until smooth.

**FLAVORINGS:**

*Vanilla:* Fold 1 tablespoon pure vanilla extract into the buttercream.

*Chocolate:* Melt 2 cups (9 ounces) chopped semisweet chocolate or semisweet chocolate morsels, let cool to room temperature and fold into buttercream until smooth.

*Coffee:* Make a coffee extract by dissolving 2 tablespoons instant coffee or espresso in 2 teaspoons hot water. Fold into the buttercream until smooth.

*Mocha:* Make chocolate buttercream and fold in coffee extract (above).

*Orange:* Fold the grated zest of 2 oranges, $1/2$ teaspoon pure orange extract and 2 tablespoons thawed, frozen orange juice concentrate into the buttercream until smooth.

*Lemon:* Fold the grated zest of 2 lemons, 1 teaspoon pure lemon extract, and 2 tablespoons fresh lemon juice into the buttercream until smooth.

---

**Rich and delicious, this sauce is excellent over ice cream, or drizzled over poached pears or pound cake.**

# CARAMEL SAUCE  Makes 1 cup

1 cup sugar

2 tablespoons water

¼ teaspoon fresh lemon juice

1 cup heavy cream

¼ teaspoon salt

2 teaspoons pure vanilla extract

1. Combine the sugar, water, and lemon juice in a heavy medium saucepan. Cook over medium heat, swirling the pan occasionally, until the sugar dissolves and starts to turn color. Increase heat to high and let the mixture bubble until it turns a rich caramel brown, swirling the pan occasionally to make sure the sugar browns evenly. This should take about 4 to 5 minutes. (If the mixture gets too brown—about the color of a dirty penny—it will start to smoke and the resulting caramel will taste burned.)

2. Remove the pan from heat and carefully stir in the cream and salt using a long-handled spoon. Be careful, as the hot caramel will hiss and spit as the cold cream hits it.

3. Reduce heat to low and cook the sauce, stirring constantly, until it thickens, about 4 to 5 minutes. Remove from heat and stir in the vanilla.

4. Let the sauce cool to room temperature before serving. To store, cover and refrigerate for up to 1 week.

This easy sauce is wonderful with profiteroles or served alone with ice cream.

# CHOCOLATE SAUCE   Makes 1 cup

8 ounces semisweet chocolate, coarsely chopped, or semisweet chocolate morsels

4 tablespoons unsalted butter, cut into small pieces

$\frac{1}{4}$ cup water

3 tablespoons light corn syrup

1 teaspoon pure vanilla extract

1. In a double boiler over simmering water, combine all the ingredients and stir constantly until the chocolate is melted and the sauce is smooth. Or, combine all the ingredients in a microwave-safe bowl and heat on high for $1\frac{1}{2}$ to 2 minutes. Remove the bowl from the microwave and stir until smooth.

2. Serve immediately, or cover and refrigerate for up to 1 week.

Note: To return chilled sauce to its liquid state, reheat in a double boiler over barely simmering water, stirring occasionally until melted. Or, place in a microwave-safe bowl and microwave on medium heat for $1\frac{1}{2}$ to 2 minutes, or until melted.

The gorgeous color and tangy flavor makes this vibrant sauce a delightful accompaniment to many desserts.

# RASPBERRY COULIS

Makes 1½ to 2 cups

1 pound frozen unsweetened raspberries, thawed

2 tablespoons sugar, or to taste

1 or 2 tablespoons Grand Marnier or other orange liqueur (optional)

1. Puree the raspberries and any accumulated juice in a blender or food processor until smooth. Using the back of a large spoon, press the puree through a fine-meshed sieve into a bowl. Discard the seeds.

2. Stir the sugar and liqueur, if using, into the puree. Taste and adjust the sweetening, if necessary. The raspberry sauce can be refrigerated for up to 1 week or frozen for up to 1 month.

This delicious icing is very easy to make and remains shiny even after being refrigerated.

# CHOCOLATE ICING

Makes 1 cup, or enough to dip 2 dozen éclairs

6 tablespoons unsalted butter

6 ounces semisweet chocolate morsels

¼ cup light corn syrup

1 teaspoon pure vanilla extract

1. In a double boiler over barely simmering water, melt the butter and chocolate with the corn syrup. Stir until smooth. Or, combine the butter, chocolate, and corn syrup in a microwave-safe bowl and heat, uncovered, on high for 1 minute. Remove from the microwave and stir to combine. Return the bowl to the microwave and heat on high for 1 more minute. Remove from the microwave and stir until very smooth and combined. Stir in the vanilla.

Make sure to dip the éclairs in this icing as soon as it is made, before it has a chance to set.

# COFFEE FONDANT ICING
Makes 1 cup, or enough to dip 2 dozen éclairs

**2 cups confectioners' sugar**

**2 tablespoons instant coffee or espresso dissolved in 2 teaspoons hot water**

**1 tablespoon warm milk**

1. Sift the sugar into a medium bowl and whisk in the coffee mixture and milk until very smooth.

**Praline is one of the basics of the French *pâtissier*, or pastry chef.** A combination of caramelized sugar and almonds or hazelnuts, praline is often pulverized and added to many traditional French desserts.

# PRALINE
Makes ¹/₂ cup crushed praline

**1 tablespoon water**

**¹/₂ cup sugar**

**¹/₂ cup slivered, blanched almonds**

1. Lightly grease a baking sheet and set aside. In a large, heavy saucepan, stir the sugar and water together until the sugar is uniformly damp and sandy. Add the almonds and cook over medium heat, swirling the pan occasionally but not stirring, until the sugar melts and turns a light golden color.

2. Remove the pan from heat and immediately pour the mixture onto the prepared pan. Let cool completely.

3. When completely cool, remove the hardened candy from the baking sheet and place in a self-sealing plastic bag. Crush the praline into a coarse powder using a large rolling pin or meat mallet.

**Sweet pastry dough, known as *pâte sucrée* in French, is a necessity for many French tarts.** Similar to sablé dough, this sweet pastry is like a delicate butter cookie rather than a traditional flaky pie dough. It is an excellent choice for tarts with sweet, creamy fillings or when a sweeter pastry shell is desired. Remember, to keep the crust tender, work with the dough as little as possible. Once the ingredients are combined, stop! This recipe makes a cookielike crust that is sturdy enough to either roll out or crumble into a pie tin and press in with your fingers. Unlike many sweet pastry doughs, this one does not need to be filled with weights while being baked.

# *S*WEET *P*ASTRY *D*OUGH    Makes one 9½-inch pastry shell

5 tablespoons unsalted butter, softened

½ cup confectioners' sugar, sifted

1 egg yolk at room temperature

½ teaspoon pure vanilla extract

¼ teaspoon salt

1¼ cups unbleached all-purpose flour

1. In a large bowl, using an electric mixer, beat the butter and sugar together until creamy. Beat in the egg yolk and vanilla. Sift the flour and salt into the butter mixture and beat at low speed just until a soft dough forms. Or, combine the butter and sugar in a food processor and pulse until combined and creamy. Add the egg yolk and vanilla and pulse to combine. Add the flour and salt and pulse just until a soft dough forms.

2. Pat the dough into a disk. Roll the pastry into an 11-inch circle between two sheets of plastic wrap or waxed paper. This keeps the pastry from sticking to the rolling pin without having to use too much flour, which can toughen the pastry.

3. Remove the top sheet of the plastic wrap or waxed paper and invert the pastry circle into the tart pan. With the second sheet of plastic wrap or waxed paper still attached to the pastry, gently ease the pastry into the shell, using your fingers to press it up against the sides of the pan without stretching the dough, allowing the excess dough to fall over the edge of the pan. Remove the plastic wrap (if the dough is too soft and the plastic wrap or waxed paper is sticking or pulling, refrigerate the dough for a few minutes to firm up before removing it). Roll the rolling pin over the top of the pan to trim the excess dough. Use a fork to generously prick the bottom of the pastry shell.

4. Cover the tart pan loosely with plastic wrap and allow it to rest in the refrigerator for at least 30 minutes. After the pastry is chilled, freeze the dough solid—at least 30 minutes. (The tart shells can be well wrapped and frozen for up to 1 week.)

## TART SHELLS

**Partially baked tart shell:** Place an oven rack on the bottom shelf of the oven. Preheat the oven to 400°F. Place the tart pan on a heavy baking sheet and bake for 10 minutes, or until the pastry is set. Should the pastry bubble up in places, simply puncture the bubbles with a fork as it bakes. Reduce the oven temperature to 375°F and continue baking for 10 to 12 minutes, or until the pastry is a pale golden brown and the interior is dry.

**Fully baked tart shell:** Bake for 10 minutes at 400°F, as above, then reduce the oven temperature to 375°F and continue baking for 15 to 18 minutes, or until the pastry is golden brown and the interior is crisp.

**Tartlet shells:** Prepare the sweet pastry dough and divide it into 4 pieces. Roll each portion into a 6-inch circle. Line four 4³/₄-inch tartlet pans with the pastry and chill as in the master recipe. Alternatively, crumble each portion of the dough into the tartlet pans and press evenly on the bottom and sides of the pan with your fingers.

**Partially baked tartlet shells:** Place the tartlet pans on a heavy baking sheet and bake at 400°F for 7 to 10 minutes, or until the pastry is set. Should the pastry bubble up in places, simply puncture the bubbles with a fork as it bakes. Reduce the oven temperature to 375°F and continue baking for 7 to 10 minutes, or until the pastry is pale golden brown and the interior is dry.

**Fully baked tartlet shells:** Bake for 7 to 10 minutes at 400°F. Reduce the oven temperature to 375°F and continue baking for 12 to 15 minutes, or until the pastry is golden brown and the interior is crisp.

A rich, tender dough full of mellow chocolate flavor.

# SWEET CHOCOLATE PASTRY

Makes one 9$\frac{1}{2}$-inch tart shell, or four 4$\frac{3}{4}$-inch tartlet shells

5 tablespoons unsalted butter, softened

$\frac{1}{2}$ cup confectioners' sugar, sifted

1 egg yolk at room temperature

$\frac{1}{2}$ teaspoon pure vanilla extract

$\frac{1}{4}$ cup unsweetened Dutch processed cocoa powder

1 cup unbleached all-purpose flour

Pinch of salt

1. In a food processor, or with an electric mixer set at low speed, mix together the butter and confectioners' sugar just until combined. Beat in the egg yolk and vanilla. Sift the cocoa, flour and salt together. Process, or beat together with the butter mixture just until a soft dough forms. Pat the dough into a disk, wrap well in plastic wrap, and chill for at least 30 minutes or up to 1 week. Proceed as for Sweet Pastry Dough (page 137).

# INDEX

# TABLE OF EQUIVALENTS

The exact equivalents in the following tables have been rounded for convenience.

**LIQUID/DRY MEASURES**

*U.S. = Metric*

$1/4$ teaspoon = 1.25 milliliters

$1/2$ teaspoon = 2.5 milliliters

1 teaspoon = 5 milliliters

1 tablespoon (3 teaspoons) =
   15 milliliters

1 fluid ounce (2 tablespoons) =
   30 milliliters

$1/4$ cup = 60 milliliters

$1/3$ cup = 80 milliliters

$1/2$ cup = 120 milliliters

1 cup   240 milliliters

1 pint (2 cups) = 480 milliliters

1 quart (4 cups, 32 ounces) =
   960 milliliters

1 gallon (4 quarts) = 3.84 liters


1 ounce (by weight) = 28 grams

1 pound = 454 grams

2.2 pounds = 1 kilogram

**LENGTH**

*U.S. = Metric*

$1/8$ inch = 3 millimeters

$1/4$ inch = 6 millimeters

$1/2$ inch = 12 millimeters

1 inch = 2.5 centimeters

**OVEN TEMPERATURE**

*Fahrenheit = Celsius = Gas*

250 = 120 = $1/2$

275 = 140 = 1

300 = 150 = 2

325 = 160 = 3

350 = 180 = 4

375 = 190 = 5

400 = 200 = 6

425 = 220 = 7

450 = 230 = 8

475 = 240 = 9

500 = 260 = 10

END
(LE FIN)

Place du Tentre, Paris, *18th arrondissement*